Scientists are still not completely certain about the role of the dust bath in the general scheme of good health care for chinchillas—but they have made some interesting observations.

# DISEASES OF CHINCHILLAS

## Prof. Dr. Helmut Kraft

# Translated by U. Erich Friese.

## *Photography and Artwork*

H.-D. DELLMANN: 42 (both), 43; ISABELLE FRANCAIS: 5, 7 (lower 2 photos), 74, 75; R. HAUPT: 64, 70, 81; R. HEBEL: 34; MICHAEL GILROY: 3, 5, 7 (upper 3 photos), 41, 143; DR. F. HOLZINGER: 72; DR. H. KEMPER: 130, 131; PROF. DR. HELMUT KRAFT: 15, 19, 32, 47, 48, 52, 55, 61, 65, 71, 77, 80, 86, 87, 88, 92, 97, 100, 105 (top), 109 (middle and bottom), 115, 116, 117 (top left); E. MOSSLACHER: 11, 79 (lower); DR. PIRELLI: 24, 25; H. POFAHL: 13, 49, 60, 63, 79 (upper), 93, 105 (bottom), 106, 107, 109 (top); M. ROSSKOPF: 39 (top right, bottom); GERHARD SCHREIBER (photo archives): 16, 23, 102, 108, 127; VINCENT SERBIN: 25; DR. P. WALTER: 37, 39 (top left), 44, 45; DR. W. ZIMMERMANN: 12, 78.

Originally published in German by Albrecht Philler Verlag under the title *Krankheiten der Chinchillas*. ©1959, 1962, 1974 by Gerhard Schreiber, München. ©1984 by Albrecht Philler Verlag, Minden.

Distributed in the UNITED STATES by T.F.H. Publications, Inc., 211 West Sylvania Avenue, Neptune City, NJ 07753; in CANADA to the Pet Trade by H & L Pet Supplies Inc., 27 Kingston Crescent, Kitchener, Ontario N2B 2T6; Rolf C. Hagen Ltd., 3225 Sartelon Street, Montreal 382 Quebec; in CANADA to the Book Trade by Macmillan of Canada (A Division of Canada Publishing Corporation), 164 Commander Boulevard, Agincourt, Ontario M1S 3C7; in ENGLAND by T.F.H. Publications Limited, 4 Kier Park, Ascot, Berkshire SL5 7DS; in AUSTRALIA AND THE SOUTH PACIFIC by T.F.H. (Australia) Pty. Ltd., Box 149, Brookvale 2100 N.S.W., Australia; in NEW ZEALAND by Ross Haines & Son, Ltd., 18 Monmouth Street, Grey Lynn, Auckland 2 New Zealand; in SINGAPORE AND MALAYSIA by MPH Distributors (S) Pte., Ltd., 601 Sims Drive, #03/07/21, Singapore 1438; in the PHILIPPINES by Bio-Research, 5 Lippay Street, San Lorenzo Village, Makati Rizal; in SOUTH AFRICA by Multipet Pty. Ltd., 30 Turners Avenue, Durban 4001. Published by T.F.H. Publications Inc. Manufactured in the United States of America by T.F.H. Publications, Inc.

# Contents

Regardless of whether chinchillas are maintained for their commercial value or maintained strictly as pets, they deserve the best care their owners can provide. Cages of wire construction are the best over-all housing units for chinchillas.

# Introductory Note

Our knowledge about chinchilla diseases still contains large gaps that, due to a lack of suitable investigative methods and materials, cannot yet be closed. In the meantime, however, there is a sizable amount of relevant literature that has been incorporated into this book. The American literature is not mentioned in great detail, since other standards and different types of medications prevail in Europe. Some American reference material, however, has been incorporated under special portions of the discussions. American readers will be able to use the information presented here, but consultation with your veterinarian will be necessary to allow for differences in drug names and certain techniques. Most of the more complicated procedures will require veterinary assistance anyway, so anyone maintaining numbers of chinchillas should have a "family" vet to call on.

Since the most common disease problems in chinchillas today are infections and diseases affecting the internal organs, the author felt qualified to write this book. The reader will appreciate that as a veterinarian I cannot deal here in detail with the particular experiences of pet owners and breeders. Yet it must also be emphasized that the information provided in this book could not have been gathered without the active support of responsive breeders. My special gratitude goes out to those who have given me their full support for this project and who helped solve problems that would have remained unsolved without their support. Beyond that, breeders are advised to deal only with those problems that they can handle within their own expertise and knowledge and not to venture into areas that have not yet been fully researched.

For the valuable help in the production of this book I would like to express my special thanks to Gerhard Schreiber.

**Prof. Dr. Helmut Kraft**
**Munich**

# 1) Care and Maintenance

## NATURAL HABITAT OF CHINCHILLAS

When we humans remove an animal from its natural habitat and force it to live among us, we are obliged to provide it with the best possible care. The basis of such care must be a knowledge and understanding of the "best possible (optimum) conditions" in the natural habitat of these animals.

During the 70's Schindler traveled through an area of the High Andes in South America where he saw chinchillas. This area is generally known to be part of the natural range of this species. He informs me that in the area of the Chacaltaya at La Paz (about 5,000 m above sea level) and in the Tumari lagoon, bedrock prevails, while the soil in the western Cordilleras of Bolivia, about 3,800 to 4,000 m, is of volcanic origin. The climatic conditions in these areas show substantial variations between day and night. Measurements taken by Schindler at La Paz during the rainy season gave -1°C to -10°C (30°-14°F) at night, and a temperature during the peak of sunshine of 50°C (122°F), usually about 30°C (86°F) at midday. On a single day the humidity was 60% 8:45 AM, 32% at noon, with a low of 4% recorded during his trip. This means that the humidity values in nature are well below those in our chinchilla facilities, as both Europe and eastern North America are very humid. Moreover, our ambient room temperatures are also generally higher than those in the natural habitat of these animals.

Plants present in this region include steppe grass (*Stipa ichu*) and Tola heather, which grow as individual clumps or bushes along the barren ground. The fauna in that region is not very diverse. Presumably birds of prey play the largest

*Chinchilla lanigera (velligera)*

role as natural enemies of chinchillas. According to my observations the reaction to large birds among chinchillas is more profound than among other mammals of similar size, which tend to ignore them. There are many ground beetles, and possibly chinchillas may well feed on the occasional insect larvae. Chinchillas live in caves under rocks; apparently they do not dig ground burrows.

These are some of the most recent ecological details known from an area where chinchillas are still being observed in their natural habitat. Unfortunately, wild chinchillas are now absent over much of their former range and are classified as endangered in several countries.

## HOUSING

We can draw some significant conclusions for the care and maintenance of our animals from these observations. Chinchillas are used to low temperatures with low relative humidity. This provides for good pelt qualities. In their natural habitat chinchillas live on hard, rocky ground, and consequently we should provide some rocks or at least hard wood as substrate in some parts of the cage. Welded mesh wire may well be hygienic, provided it is kept clean, but in the long term this is not healthy for the feet of our animals. Since chinchillas live in caves in their natural habitat we must give them similar opportunities in captivity, so their accommodations must include similar hiding places. Finally, it is in the nature of chinchillas to jump, therefore cages with several built-in levels have proven to be very useful.

Species-correct care also includes continuous observation of our animals. Only through close monitoring of their behavior toward each other can we recognize the state of their well-being. From this we get to know our animals intimately and we can help them to remain healthy and contented.

One particular aspect that is of greatest significance for correct care is the size and type of cage used. There is a whole variety of cages commercially available, but some chinchilla breeders make their own. Quite fundamentally, we have to distinguish between breeding cages and those used to house pet animals.

The minimal dimensions for holding cages for single pets given access to play areas must be such that a fully grown chinchilla can move about in it with ease. The smallest cages

*Chinchilla brevicaudata (boliviana)*

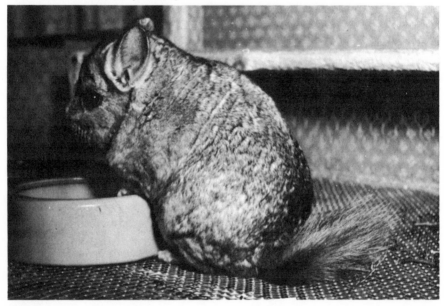

Chinchilla with "goat back." Animals like this are always suspected of being disease carriers (gastrointestinal tract, liver, etc.).

must not be cluttered with dust baths, shelters, and resting boards or perches so that the animal must constantly hop up and down and can no longer move about unobstructed along the floor. While it may be advantageous to have a built-in dust bath, this also does have its disadvantages: it takes up a lot of space and the animal quickly gnaws through the lid so that the dust bath becomes soiled with feces and food remnants. In my experience this has not proved to be successful. The smallest possible holding cage would be 40 x 40 x 40 cm (16 x 16 x 16 inches).

In respect to breeding cages, one has to remember that these are used for long-term holding of two adult animals and often two or three times a year also for one to three young. This applies to both monogamous and polygamous breeding. Although under polygamous conditions the buck is only temporarily together with the female, the dimensions nevertheless have to be the same as for a monogamous cage. Therefore, the *minimum dimensions* for a breeding cage are 50 x 50 x 60 cm (20 x 20 x 24 inches).

## NUTRITION

One of the most important factors for proper chinchilla care is nutrition. Chinchillas are rodents; they have well-developed, strong gnawing teeth (incisors) in the front of the upper and lower jaw and heavy molar teeth at the back that are built to grind food. Feeding tends to wear down the incisor teeth and the molars if proper food to chew is provided. If this particular point is neglected it can lead to substantial dental changes, which then by necessity affect the overall well-being of the animals. Chinchillas like to gnaw on porous rocks and fruit tree branches. As far as the latter is concerned, however, it must be emphasized that today most fruit trees are sprayed with insecticides that can be as poisonous to mammals as they are to insects! These harmful chemicals weaken the body even if they do not kill, and the next time the chinchilla is exposed to disease-causing germs or other stress the animal may not have enough resistance to fend off a disease.

A second important factor in the nutrition of chinchillas is that these animals are herbivorous (plant-feeders), which is reflected in their body structure. For instance, the stomach and intestinal tract of a chinchilla with a length of 20 cm from top of head to tip of tail is 2.5 m long, including stomach and cecum, both of which are relatively large. There are considerable similarities between the digestive tracts of horses and chinchillas. From this we conclude that our animals must be given a type of food that contains sufficient roughage. To give a high-energy diet alone is wrong. Similarly unsuitable, in my opinion, is alfalfa hay. We know that it is very energy-rich, but according to the natural habitat of these animals they are adapted to a low-energy food. I believe good quality meadow hay is very suitable, and where possible highland or alpine hay should be used.

In general, it can be said that chinchillas require good quality food just as do other animals. In regard to food, chin-

**Above:** Chinchilla feeding on white bread given as a tidbit. **Below:** Feeding heartily.

chillas are neither more nor less sensitive than other animals — or man, for that matter. Individual specimens always react "individually," but usually chinchillas are just as affected by natural or chemical poisons as is man. Here it should be remembered that foods, food additives, medica-

15

Dried meadow saffron with fruit capsules and leaves as found in hay with a conspicuous brownish coloration.

tions, vitamins and hormones can act as "poisons" when they are given as an overdose or, for that matter, as an underdose. The old saying "plenty helps plenty" is as wrong when applied to chinchillas as it is under other circumstances. In addition, for each animal species there are specific food substances that can be harmful, but through experience we learn to recognize and eliminate them. Everybody must acquire this sort of experience himself rather than by just relying on the effort of others, and explicit findings and observations should be published for the benefit of all those who keep chinchillas.

Constant observations and control of diets will also lead the way toward improving the nutrition of chinchillas in captivity. Close monitoring of the digestive process from food in-

16

take to bowel movements will quickly point out any mistakes that are being made. Much has been written about the "normal" feces or droppings of chinchillas. Here again individual variations and peculiarities must be expected and taken into consideration. The feces must be of a shape and consistency typical for chinchillas: it must be dry and of a brownish greenish color. Beyond that, the type of food given and the fluid intake play a significant part in the color and consistency of the droppings. This then makes it somewhat presumptuous to talk about "normal" droppings. Those who have seen many different chinchilla stocks will agree that even animals with "abnormal" droppings can attain a substantial longevity. However, feces with drawn-out, pointed ends and with a slimy coating is always an ominous sign of digestive disorder.

Regardless of all those publications that report that the nutrition of chinchillas no longer presents a problem, it appears relevant to make some comments about feeding and diets. Many different feeding recipes have been recommended in recent decades. One experienced breeder recommends a mixed food diet along the following lines:

**Main feeding (evening)**
1 tablespoon pellets per animal
1 bottle fresh drinking water
1 handful hay (first cut)

**Feeding in the morning**
½ tablespoon mixed food, consisting of:
3 kg wheat bran, coarse
3 kg oats
3 kg barley
1 kg millet
½ kg linseed
½ kg dietary calcium, commercial
½ kg salt
200 g fennel
1 pkt skimmed milk powder (200 g)
1 bottle fresh drinking water
1 handful hay (first cut)

In addition, each animal gets a thumb-sized piece of dried bread. The following mixture of herbs (dried and macerated by hand) is added to the above mixed food:

3 heaped tablespoons chamomille
3 heaped tablespoons hips
2 heaped tablespoons peppermint
1 heaped tablespoon sage
½ heaped tablespoon St. John's wort

The food mixture, made up of these ingredients, gives about 15 kg, which is sufficient for 100 animals. It lasts for about eight to ten weeks and should be stored dry and cool, so that it is always fresh when used. If there are fewer animals the individual ingredients can be prorated by using only ½, ⅓, ¼, etc.

Another recipe advocated by some breeders consists of:

100 g wheat bran
50 g wheat germ
15 g yeast
15 g barley flour
10 g linseed

It is recommended to add some vitamins and possibly also some liquid such as water, milk or fruit or vegetable juices (diluted).

Roughage such as hay, oat straw, bean straw or pea straw must be given.

An endless array of recipes could be listed here, most of which are really no longer of interest, because the progressive breeder will simply feed pellets, hay, and water to his chinchillas. If this is done properly there is very little that can go wrong — but this diet is not foolproof.

Here it may be relevant to mention a special diet for sick chinchillas. It is composed of:

10 tablespoons oatmeal
5 tablespoons alfalfa hay meal or straw meal
1 tablespoon ground linseed
1 tablespoon dried yeast (coarse)
1 tablespoon glucose
1 tablespoon dietary calcium product
2 tablespoons rice flakes (hulled)
½ tablespoon skimmed milk powder

Apart from this special diet there are also a number of recipes for rearing young and for pregnant and nursing females.

Here is only one example from the multitude of material available.

It was once reported that pregnant and nursing females should largely be fed the same way as other females, except that they should be given slightly more concentrated (high-energy) food — grain, yogurt, or pellets. The young that may have to be given supplementary food or are reared artificially should be given three to six times per day (depending upon their age), one part condensed milk and one part water. If desired, one can add a pinch (tip of a knife blade) of honey or glucose, but this is not absolutely necessary. According to the originator of this diet, condensed milk must be used because according to his information, normal chinchilla milk contains 15% more fat than normal cow's milk; that is, one has to produce a very high percentage of fat content in the milk so that it can be equated with chinchilla milk.

This is only a very small selection of what has appeared in the literature in recent decades on food and feeding recom-

Typically herbivorous intestinal tract of *Chinchilla lanigera*. Body length, 26 cm; intestinal tract (without stomach), 300 cm.

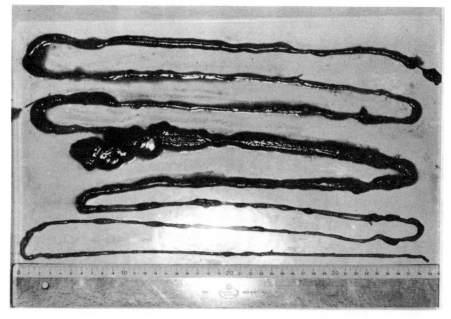

mendations for chinchillas. These are not recommendations made by commercial food manufacturers! It is important that this is kept in mind. Manufacturers would, of course, recommend food products and dietary formulas that correspond to the composition of their own products. This is particularly true for pellets. The current trend in animal mass production is to operate as cost and labor effective as possible, and the use of pellets achieves both.

There is now a wide assortment of chinchilla pellets on the market. There are also a number of manufacturers who specialize in chinchilla pellets. Each uses his own special formula. Some fundamentally important remarks must be made here: the content of nutritional ingredients is of course of decisive significance when feeding pellets. Therefore, it is important to check which basic ingredients are used in the manufacture of this compressed food. On the other hand, it is not too terribly important to know what the vitamin content is, particularly after the pellets have been stored for some time. Experience has shown that the vitamin content in such pellets only lasts for a short period of time.

In regard to the digestive compatibility of chinchilla pellets from different manufacturers, it can be said that the pellets generally are compatible, but problems do tend to occur when there is a change from one brand to another. Sometimes such a change may be needed, but in other cases it may have been due only to good salesmanship, in spite of the fact that a particular breeder may have been quite satisfied with his previous brand of pellets.

Chinchilla breeders must be cautious when changing from one pellet brand to another. Any such change must be done slowly and with great deliberation since there are inherent dangers that sometimes can have fatal consequences. Afterward it is extremely difficult to seek legal redress against pellet manufacturers, particularly so since under these circumstances it would not have involved spoiled food and the formula used for making these pellets is flawless.

Experience during the last few years has shown that in some cases it is necessary to do some pre-feeding trials when a change-over of pellets is contemplated. This needs to involve only a few animals taken from a breeding group not

20

known to be sensitive to dietary changes. These animals are fed the new pellets for a while in order to see how they handle the new food.

Basically, it can be said that optimal nutrition for our chinchillas today consists of pellets, hay, and water. It is important that these pellets are from a reputable manufacturer and that they correspond in ingredients — which must be listed on each pellet sac — to the nutritional requirements of chinchillas. Moreover, chinchilla pellets must be fresh. Each pellet sac must bear the date of manufacture.

### Yellow fat

It is not too uncommon to find a sort of fatty yellow substance along the back or abdominal musculature in skinned chinchillas. This indeed is fat that does not have the expected wax-white color. If the abdominal cavity is then opened up the internal fat is also yellow, yet the musculature (flesh) and the organs unchanged in color and consistency. Here we are dealing with "yellow fat," a lipometabolism disorder. As far as I know this has not yet been researched in chinchillas, but there is some information about "yellow fat" in mink. It occurs when a diet deficient in vitamin A is fed and leads to an abnormal oxidation of fatty deposits into yellow fat with a wax-like consistency. Similarly, the uptake of too much unsaturated fatty acids in the diet (such as rancid wheat germ) can lead to such changes. In addition, it is not too uncommon to find "watery" tissue in animals afflicted with yellow fat; often these particular animals are well developed and quite fat. Since the connective tissue fat is also affected by this color change, the pelts from chinchillas with "yellow fat" are usually unsuitable for tanning and are hardly salable.

Not all animals in a particular group or colony are affected by this metabolic disorder, and therefore breeders generally do not believe that the diet is at fault. Each animal reacts individually since physiological conditions vary from one chinchilla to the next. "Yellow ears" can be an externally visible sign of "yellow fat."

As a preventive measure, breeders should make sure that their animals always get enough vitamins E and A. Usually the full vitamin requirements are NOT met by the principal diet alone and there will have to be vitamin supplements administered. If wheat germ is used, it is important to make sure that the grains are not rancid, the prime cause for the development of unsaturated fatty acids. Storage in excess of eight to 14 days is not recommended. Moreover, the breeder has to make sure when he is feeding pellets that unsaturated acids have not developed during compaction of the pellets. This is of course only applicable if ingredients that can give off unsaturated acids when heated are being used in the manufacture of chinchilla pellets.

**Water budget**

A much-discussed topic among chinchilla breeders is the liquid uptake. The opinions vary from "lots of water" to "no water at all." Both of these extremes are surely wrong. There is no animal that can live without liquid uptake, but many animals can get all required liquid from their food, provided the food contains enough liquid. If animals are fed only on pressed or dried foods they cannot sufficiently balance their water budget, but if occasionally a few pieces of apple are also given, a large amount of the required liquid can be obtained this way. Nevertheless, chinchillas should be offered clean, fresh water daily. Close monitoring of the animals will soon indicate how much they are drinking. It is not the amount of water taken in that is important, but the quality of the water.

Zimmermann has made some theoretical calculations in regard to the water budget of chinchillas. Based on the water requirements of humans, a chinchilla weighing 500 g gives off the following volumes of water during a 24-hour period: in urine: 10 ml 55.5%; via the skin: 3 ml 16.7%; via the lungs: 4 ml 22.2%; in feces: 1 ml 5.6%. Consequently, a fully grown chinchilla gives off 18 ml of water in a 24-hour period and so the same volume will have to be replenished.

My own observations were confined exclusively to food and water intake and the loss of liquid via urine and feces. The animals (average weight 440 g) were kept in the same room for the entire period (summer and winter) at a temperature of 18° to 20°C (65-68°F) and a relative humidity of 50 to 60%. The main diet consisted of hay, grain, and a mineral

22

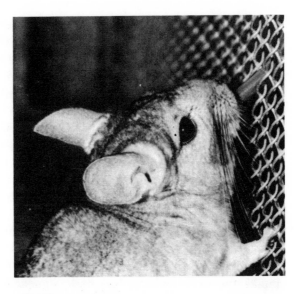

Chinchilla drinking from bottle.

salt mixture. During the first 18 months (first test period) the chinchillas were given the above-mentioned dried foods, once or twice a week a slice of apple, and daily about 20 ml of drinking water. Food and drinking water were nearly always completely taken. During this test period the animals passed urine daily (once or twice) and produced the usual amount of feces (on the average, 3-5 g in a 24-hour period).

During the second test period the animals were not given any water. Instead, this was replaced by the water content of the food. The usual "dried food" was supplemented by apples, oranges, mandarins, and other fruits. During the summer and for as long as possible (more than six months) I also gave daily freshly cut green food (one handful of grass per animal). Since the grass was usually covered with dew it had a high water content. During this period the experimental animals passed urine once to three times a day and the feces was relatively wet but still properly shaped. Possible detrimental influences of the drinking water such as chlorine content and pollution can be avoided this way, but this diet has a severe effect on the intestinal function. Although none of my experimental animals fell ill, there was an increased danger of intestinal infections.

After water had been withheld completely for one year the animals were fed again as during the first experimental period. During this third and final experimental phase they were also given 50 ml tap water per animal every other day. The urine was collected in small glass dishes and measured, and the feces samples were checked for their water content. Collecting urine from chinchillas presents hardly any difficulties since these animals always urinate at the same location in their cage. A glass dish placed under the wire mesh bottom and checked every three to five hours always contains only one entire urine volume or none at all. In order to obtain random feces samples the cage was completely cleaned and then the droppings were removed after 12 or 14 hours. Of course, the dust in the bath also had to be sifted.

These experiments revealed that my chinchillas would take up 40 to 50 ml of water within a 24-hour period when 50 ml of water was provided every other day. On the days of water intake the urine volume was understandably larger than on "water free" days. According to my experimental results, *Chinchilla lanigera* passes about 0.5 to 1 ml of urine at a time, with a daily urine volume of 1 to 2 ml. If a lot of water is taken the individual urine volume may increase up to 3 ml and the daily volume up to 12 ml. This natural process of diuresis (increase of urine formation and passage) occurs during the first five hours after liquid uptake and lasts for about 24 hours.

With the usual dry diet and water supplements of up to 20 ml daily, the feces contain 9-10% liquid. This corresponds to 0.3 to 0.5 ml water with a daily amount of 3 to 5 g of feces per animal. When more liquid was given one could readily detect an increased moisture content in the feces of some chinchillas.

These experiments show that chinchillas take up a substantial amount of water if it is available to them. They react to it by passing an increased volume of urine, just as do other mammals. When water is withdrawn the animals pass correspondingly less urine and the feces are drier than usual. For technical reasons I was unable to ascertain where else (through what other body parts) water is given off by chinchillas and how it is given off.

In reference to diseases and their diagnosis it can be said that we can easily monitor the urine of chinchillas. More-

The water bottle suspended at one side of the cage shown here allows the cage's inhabitant to drink as much as it wants. Water must of course be maintained in a permanently clean and fresh condition.

over, it appears obvious that the supply of liquid in volumes greater than 20 ml per animal per day included in food or as drinking water places an increased burden on the digestive and urinary tracts, leading to an increased susceptibility to diseases.

25

# 2) Hygiene

Hygiene can also be described as cleanliness. There are animals that are already clean in their behavior and mannerisms, such as cats. In my opinion chinchillas are also clean and immaculate animals, but we can not expect them to keep their wooden or metal "cave" clean. They are unfamiliar with the material and form. Here we have to intervene. We must make sure that their cage is not only clean but that it stays that way.

Location of cages and enclosures is part of hygiene. They must not be located in drafty or damp rooms. They have to be constructed in such a way that they are easy to clean, and the bedding tray must be maintained in such a way that moisture is always soaked up with sawdust, wood shavings, or newspaper. Food dishes must be cleaned every day because even the smallest amount of uneaten food can quickly spoil, turn sour, and start to fungus, causing diseases.

Even closer attention has to be paid to cleaning the "artificial caves" (shelters). They have a multitude of cracks and gaps that can easily harbor disease germs if not cleaned thoroughly. If there are sick animals around they must be separated from the main group. There must also be separate sets of cleaning and service tools and equipment. If animals die or if new animals are introduced into a previously occupied cage, this cage must first be thoroughly disinfected. A variety of common household disinfectants are adequate. If one wants to be absolutely sure, the cage can be "burned out" with a blow-torch which kills even the most resistant germs.

If new animals are purchased it is advisable to keep these isolated for a few weeks. A quarantine cage should be part of every modern chinchilla facility.

## DUST BATHS

One specific hygiene requirement for chinchillas is a dust bath. It serves to cleanse, massage, and care for the animal's pelt. Again, what has been said before about observing the animals also applies here. Close monitoring quickly reveals how the animals take to this bath and how they behave in the bath. It goes without saying that this bath must not contain any poisonous substances (such as disinfectants) since the animals sometimes eat some dust. For instance, I once found that flowers of sulphur had been added to the bath — the autopsy of a dead animal that had used this bath revealed that it had died of severe constipation. This constipation had not responded to medications, and the digestive tract still contained flowers of sulphur.

## DEATHS

Life starts with birth and ends with death. Between these two extremes is a more or less pleasant segment of life that is influenced by many things. It is an unwritten law of nature that life must end some day, either earlier or later. Up to now we are still not able to give an exact average maximum age for chinchillas, but we know that this is about eight years. Therefore, it is a natural process when animals occasionally die. It is also within normal probabilities that where many animals live together more events occur than at a place where one finds only individual units. Transposed to our chinchilla breeding activities, this means that large animal aggregations will produce more deaths than smaller ones, and that disease problems at least tend to be more diverse in larger facilities than in smaller stocks, provided, of course, that the owners of both types of facilities are "breeders" and they understand the ground rules of animal husbandry and animal breeding. In other words, there is really no need to panic if suddenly one or more animals die. There are always losses, but the cause does not always need to be a disease or an epidemic! A close assessment of the situation and a detailed autopsy of the dead animals made by a veterinarian or at a specialized facility are the only possibilities to determine the cause, if it is indeed possible at all. The breeder must attempt — objectively — to remove any deficiencies in his operation, and the veterinarian will handle the medical veterinary aspects of it. For many breeders this has already proved to be a good practice, and it would indeed be desirable if this sort of cooperation would spread further through the chinchilla breeding community.

In any event, a death in the colony is always a warning sign, and it would certainly be wrong to dismiss this entirely on the grounds that deaths happen. Close scrutiny of the overall situation will indicate whether this is a "biological" death or if it is indeed a disease problem. If in doubt, the dead animal should be taken for an autopsy. This service is never free of charge, but the costs involved are within reasonable limits. After all, the examination results benefit the entire stock, and the earlier a disease is diagnosed the easier it is to treat it effectively. If one waits until several chinchillas are dead the pathogen may have spread widely through the colony so that too many animals are already infected for any treatment to be successful.

## QUARANTINE

Quarantine, originally a 40-day isolation and observation period of animals suspected of carrying infectious pathogens, is one of the most effective disease prevention measures in animal husbandry. It protects animal stocks against an introduction of infectious diseases and limits the progress of a disease. Quarantine must be viewed from two different vantage points:

— what belongs in quarantine, and
— how to set up a quarantine facility.

All newly purchased animals that could conceivably be carriers of infectious disease without actually showing any symptoms must initially be placed into quarantine. The mere change of environment can cause a disease to break out or the "new" germs may cause diseases among established stock.

All obviously sick animals must be quarantined as long as the majority of the stock is still healthy. This procedure can also be designated as a transfer to an "isolation station." It goes without saying that all chinchillas already in quarantine have to be kept isolated from other new acquisitions.

When setting up a quarantine facility we have to remember

that this is to be a "true" quarantine! The animals to be isolated have to be accommodated in a separate room in clean, disinfected cages. The animals themselves must be kept as usual so that there are no additional stress factors: that is, humidity, temperature, caging, food, and drinking water must be the same as for the main animal stock unless a special diet is called for. Clearly all food and food containers used in the quarantine facility must be kept separate from those used elsewhere.

When newly purchased chinchillas are kept in quarantine, they should be fed *before* the main stock is fed. If the quarantine station is operated as an isolation station and is occupied by sick animals or those suspected to be sick, these should be taken care of *after* the main stock has been fed.

Anyone moving from quarantine to the breeding facility and in reverse must wash and disinfect his/her hands thoroughly. A change of working (protective) clothing is also recommended.

There are no generally valid data available about the duration of a quarantine period. The original 40-day isolation was based on the experience that all infectious disease become acute during this time interval. Nowadays this can no longer be scientifically supported in every case, but a quarantine period of four to five weeks gives the best guarantee against an outbreak of a chain of infections. Depending upon the individual situation, eight to 14 days may also be sufficient. Close observation of the animals during this period will also provide valuable clues about their condition and progress.

# 3) Anatomy

In Germany during the 1950's, at the time when chinchilla breeding grew avalanche-like, there was hardly anything known about this little fur-bearing animal. Therefore, it is to the distinguished credit of Walter and his co-workers that they conducted systematic investigations, collected all relevant literature, and provided an almost complete description of the anatomy of chinchillas. Let me briefly discuss here those details where chinchillas deviate from other animal species or their respective organ groups. This may give the reader the opportunity to establish an accurate diagnosis in case of a disease typical of particular parts of the body or of organ systems.

Head and chest X-ray of chinchilla (dorsoventral penetration).

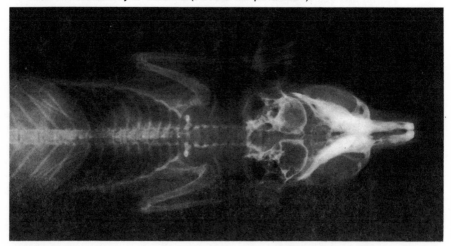

## EXTERNAL ANATOMY

Some anatomical characteristics of chinchillas are externally visible. Large sensory organs, such as eyes and ears, define the shape of the head. Extremely long tactile hairs (whiskers) protrude laterally and forward from both sides of the upper lip. The very short front legs serve both as support and to hold the food and are in distinct contrast to the large, strongly muscular posterior jumping legs. A dense, soft fur evenly covers the entire body, with up to 30 individual hairs from each hair root.

The skeleton and musculature of the locomotory apparatus of chinchillas have been studied and compared to those of nutria and rabbit, with most similarity being found to be with nutria. There are few substantial differences between the muscles of chinchillas and other rodents except those attached to the collar bone.

Chinchillas have four toes (numbers 2, 3, 4, 5 — toe 1 is lost) on their front paws and three (2, 3, 4) of different sizes on their hind paws. The first and fifth toes on the hind legs are only rudimentary.

Of the head muscles the *M. masseter* is the most developed followed by those muscles that move the ears. The *M. transversus mandibulae* is present in young but absent in fully grown chinchillas.

## DIGESTIVE TRACT

Food intake and digestion start in the oral cavity, which is rather narrow in chinchillas and largely filled by the tongue. In conjunction with digestion, the teeth are of particular interest. The dental formula is as follows:

$^1/_1$ Incisors, $^0/_0$ Canines, $^1/_1$ Premolars, $^3/_3$ Molars.

A fully grown chinchilla has four incisors and 16 molar-type teeth. The upper incisors nearly always have a right angle indentation, while the lower incisors are ground down like a pointed chisel. Cutting teeth as well as grinding teeth have open roots and therefore grow continuously. Only correct tooth position assures that the teeth are constantly being ground down. Incisors protrude for about one third of their length from the jaw and are reddish yellow.

Size and shape show distinct species differences between

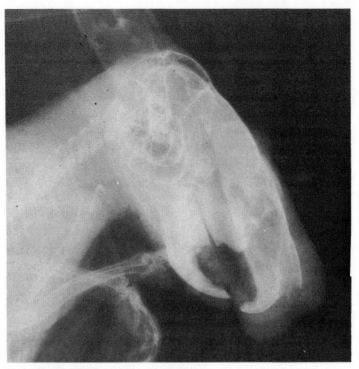

X-ray of chinchilla head (lateral penetration).

*C. brevicaudata* and *C. lanigera*. Both species have a rather large head (relative to body size), but in *C. brevicaudata* it is larger still than in *C. lanigera*. The latter, however, has a skull that is more strongly flattened than that of *C. brevicaudata*.

The skull is formed primarily by the space for the large sensory organs (eyes, ears), for a large brain, and by points of attachment for the large chewing muscles. Apart from opening the mouth, the lower jaw can only move in the longitudinal direction of the skull.

The tongue has been described as being trapezoidal in cross (transverse) section, with the two lateral areas wider than the dorsal side. The very short (relative to the total length of the tongue) dorsal fold is, in comparison to that of ruminants, flatter and moved further toward the trachea. At

32

the position corresponding to that of the lyssa in dogs one finds on the chinchilla tongue a circular fat plug. The hyoid forms a triangular bony structure.

Type and arrangement of papillae give the chinchilla tongue its specific character. In the majority of the *Papillae filiformes* the horny tips are split into several threads. Moreover, there are also *P. conicae* present just as in ruminants, but in chinchillas they have long, needle-like horny structures pointing backward toward the trachea. In addition, the chinchilla tongue also carries *P. fingiformes, P. vallatae,* and the typically well-developed marginal tongue organ. The walled-in papillae deviate from the classical from since the papilla body has become strongly elongated. The marginal tongue organ also is formed differently in chinchillas than in other domesticated animals.

The palatal ridges along the roof of the oral cavity are individually specific in chinchillas — each animal, even if closely related to another, has distinctively shaped palatal ridges that distinguish it from any other chinchilla.

The stomach in chinchillas is located completely in the thoracic cavity behind the diaphragm. In its shape it resembles that of pigs or horses; indeed, the entire digestive tract has much similarity to that of the horse. To the left and cranial to the opening of the esophagus into the stomach there is a nearly thimble-size diverticulum. The small and large curvatures of the stomach are only moderately defined in chinchillas. The pylorus can be recognized externally by a shallow constriction and is located along the right chest wall about halfway up the trunk. The musculature *(Tunica muscularis)* of the stomach at the pylorus is strengthened into a ring-like swelling, especially its inner, more circular layer. The increase in thickness starts gradually from the side of the stomach; toward the duodenum it decreases again rapidly.

The duodenum receives several afferent ducts from the pancreas, with the bile duct being at the *Papilla duodeni.* The jejunum is the longest section of the small intestine and nearly fills the entire abdominal cavity, together with sections of the large intestine. It is distinguished from the large intestine by its smooth wall. The ileum (about 3.5 cm long) forms the transition to the cecum.

As in other rodents, the cecum (blind gut) in chinchillas is located in the left half of the abdominal cavity, and due to its considerable development it occupies a substantial portion of the abdominal cavity. Under normal physiological conditions its content is small and of liquid consistency. The opening of the ileum is in the area of the caudal pole of the left kidney. From there the cecum extends forward and its tip reaches the stomach wall. It has the form of an irregular cone.

The large intestine is the intestinal segment with the greatest volume. The longest section (*Colon ascendens*) of it continues from the cecum and fills the lower half of the abdominal cavity. The posterior section of the large intestine and the rectum are filled with compacted fecal matter that can be felt through a relaxed abdominal wall.

The rectum starts in the vicinity of the kidneys without distinct delineation from the colon and progresses on the left of the median line along the dorsal abdominal wall into the pelvic cavity. Its terminal segment widens into the shape of an ampul in the region of the exit of the pelvic cavity. The anal opening, which terminates over a low hump, has radiat-

Schematic representation of fore- and hind-gut of a chinchilla (after Hebel): 1) Esophagus; 2) Stomach; 3) Blind sac of stomach; 4) Pylorus; 5) S-shaped loop of duodenum; 6) Flexura I duodeni; 7) Duodenum descendens; 8) Flexura II duodeni; 9) Duodenum transversum; 10) Flexura III duodeni; 11) Duodenum ascendens; 12) Jejunum; 13) Ileum; 14) Ileocecal uvula; 15) Cecum; 16) Colon ascendens (wide section); 17) Colon ascendens (narrow section); 18) Transition from wide to narrow section; 19) Colon transversum; 20) Colon descendens; 21) Rectum; 22) Rectal ampulla; a) Plica ileo-caecalis; b) Plica caeco-colica; c) Plica intercolica I; d) Plica intercolica II; e) Plica duodeno-colica; o) Papilla duodeni; x) Opening of Ductus pancreatus minor

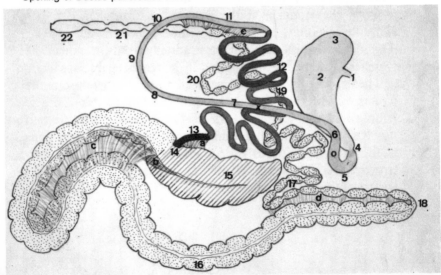

ing skin folds that terminate in hair-covered outer skin. The posterior end of the ampul is surrounded by ring-like glandular packets that in females appear to be thickened ventrally toward the vaginal roof; those in males have twice the circumference of those in females.

Although the three main elements of the mesentery are essentially confluent, they can be distinguished. The large net (retinaculum) is formed by the cranial end of the suspending mesentery of the duodenum, cecum, and a section of the colon. The second part is the relatively large mesojejunum, and the third part is the serosa plate, which serves to suspend the terminal section of the colon and the rectum. The fatty deposits are highly variable. The regional intestinal lymph nodes are located in the adjacent section of the mesentery. Apart from these suspension bands there are also mesentery bands between intestinal segments. For instance, a band extends from the *Duodenum ascendens* toward the terminal segment of the small colon, a triangular band plate lies between ileum and cecum, and another triangular band extends from the cecum toward the beginning segment of the colon. The wall structure of the digestive tract in chinchillas has principally the same sequence of layers as in other mammals.

The liver in fully grown chinchillas weighs 8 to 10 g. It is located intrathoracically between the diaphragm and stomach. At the top right it reaches the kidney and suprarenal body. The gall bladder, which is about 1 cm in size, is located between the median and right sides of the liver. There is hardly any lobulation visible over the surface of the liver. Histologically the poor development of interstitial connective tissue is conspicuous.

The pancreas (here *Pancreas difusum*) is strongly lobed. The right lobe (about 3.5 cm long) is embedded in the dorsal mesentery of the duodenum. An approximately 5-cm-long and 3-cm-wide lobe of this gland covers — embedded in the large mesentery net — the left posterior half of the stomach. A narrow, approximately 2.5-cm-long strand branches off this lobe at the level of the stomach opening and extends along the right half of the stomach adjacent to the large curvature. The *Caput pancreatis* (head of pancreas) is situated left of the beginning of the duodenum, at about the level of

35

the *Papilla duodeni*. Because of the strongly lobate condition of this organ and its extensive branches it is difficult to distinguish clearly with the naked eye between pancreatic tissue, the adjacent ample fatty tissue, and the lymph nodes in the same area. The islets of Langerhans are similar to those in guinea pigs and can be described as an incomplete mantle islet.

In chinchillas, the spleen which is triangular in cross section, belongs to the immunization type on the basis of its structure. It has the shape of a boot, whereby the "sole" is located at about the level of the next to last rib on the left side. The "tip of the boot" points upward, the "heel" downwards and to the back, and the "shaft" points forward. With its right surface area the spleen — because of the bent origin of the splenoid net — is adjacent to the left kidney. Net origin and hilus can be found at the obtuse angle of the spleen cross section; at the anterior and posterior end of the net origin line a short band extends to the kidney.

The arterial blood supply to the abdominal and pelvic organs shows some difference in comparison to the situation in other rodents previously studied. The *A. colica* and *A. colica media* originate in a joint stem. In general, chinchillas have only six strong jejunal arteries, but two cecal vessels, one dorsal and one ventral *A. caecalis*. The *A. mesenterica caudalis* protrudes only for a few millimeters from the *Aorta abdominalis*, caudally from the left kidney artery. The *A. testicularis* and *A. varica* originate from the *A. renalis*.

**Respiratory organs**

Adjacent to the outer side of each slit-like nostril there is also a "false" nostril. The anterior part of each rather large nasal cavity is arched upward. The cavities are inter-connected along their upper sections. The side cavities are accessible from the main nasal cavities via relatively large openings.

The larynx contains a small lateral pouch in the form of an indentation between vocal and pouch cords.

The dorso-ventrally compressed trachea contains many irregularly arranged mucosal pockets, especially in its proximal section. Between its clasped ends the distal tracheal section

Female sex organs: a)
Right kidney; b) Ovary; c)
Right uterine horn; d)
Ureter; e) Intestinal
convolutions; f) Liver; g)
Left kidney; h) Ovary; i)
Left uterine horn; j)
Rectum (with feces ball);
k) Cervix; l) Urinary
bladder

a
b

c

d

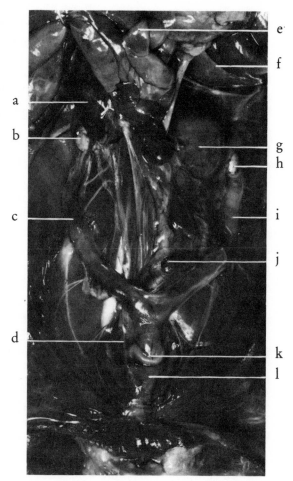

e
f

g
h

i

j

k
l

has pacchionian (meningeal) granules. Separation of the trachea occurs at the level of the fourth to fifth thoracic
vertebrae.

The lung has on its right side an apical lobe as well as a
cardiac lobe, an appendage, and a basal lobe, while the left
side has only an apical lobe, a cardiac lobe, and a basal lobe.

**Female sex organs**

The ovaries are about wheat-grain size (.3 g). They are located at or below the respective posterior kidney pole. In immature chinchillas the surface of the ovaries is smooth, but
the ovaries of sexually mature females have small gray lumps

37

that give the surface an uneven appearance. Delicate tissue connect the ovaries with the inner lumbar muscles as well as with the uterus. In chinchillas several egg cells usually mature at the same time, and during their growth period they migrate to the surface and so cause the lumpy structure. When the vesicles burst the mature eggs reach the oviduct. Consequently, several eggs can always be fertilized at the same time. When sectioned and stained, the interstitial cells can be separated into *Theca folliculi* and the cells of the stroma.

The thread-like oviduct starts at the ovaries with a funnel-shaped, frayed opening. It winds elaborately past the ovaries and then — in conjunction with suspending mesentery of the ovaries and its own connecting tissue to the inner lumbar muscles — forms the so-called ovarian pouch. In contrast to other mammals the eggs in chinchillas are not dumped into this pouch but instead remain in one wall of the pouch. The ampul-like enlargement of the oviduct has an especially strongly developed longitudinal fold. This is where the egg cells are fertilized. After that, muscles in the wall of the oviduct transport the fertilized egg cells by means of peristaltic action into the uterus.

The uterus, which starts as two horns about 6 cm long just behind the ovaries, descends posteriorly to the pelvic cavity. Chinchillas have a so-called duplex uterus in which the uterine horns as well as the uterus proper are set up in duplicate and are completely separate from each other, extending up to the mouth of the uterus. Consequently the vagina shows two openings at the mouth of the uterus.

The uterus is suspended by delicate tissues from the right and left of the upper abdominal wall. This tissue spreads just in front of the cervix and between the two uterine horns. When the uterus is closed, a so-called vaginal plug is located at the cervix; when the female comes into estrus this plug is expelled.

The sex tract terminates with the approximately 15-mm-long vagina, which becomes visible when the animal is in "heat" as a horizontal slit between the anal opening and the urethral cone. The dermal cone between the vagina and urethral cone is supported by a small bone. In female chinchillas

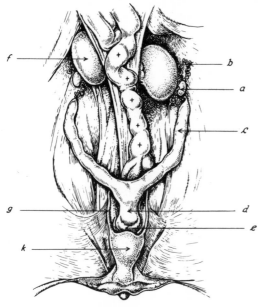

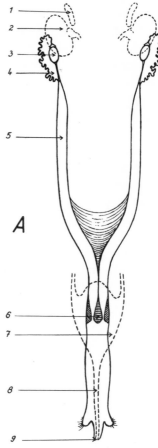

**Above:** Position of female sex organs in chinchillas: a) Ovary; b) Oviduct (Fallopian tube); c) Uterine horn; d) External view of uterus; e) Cervix; f) Kidney; g) Ureter; k) Urinary bladder and rectum.
**Above right:** Schematic representation of female sex organs in chinchillas (after Rosskopf, 1961): 1) Suprarenal; 2) Kidney; 3) Ovary; 4) Oviduct; 5) Uterus; 6) Cervix; 7) Urinary bladder; 8) Ureter; 9) Opening of vulva.

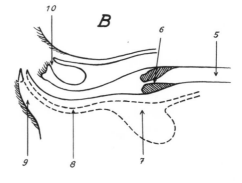

Chinchilla female sex organs (schematic lateral view) (after Rosskopf, 1961): 5) Uterus; 6) Cervix; 7) Urinary bladder; 8) Ureter; 9) Opening of vulva; 10) Anus.

39

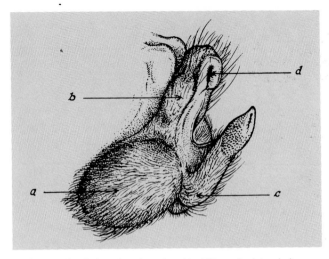

**Above:** Genital-anal region of a chinchilla male; lateral view from posterior left: a) Testicle pouch; b) Epididymal pouch; c) Penis (second bend in foreskin pocket): d) Anus (after Dellmann, 1962). **Below:** Schematic view of male genitalia: 1) Epididymus and sperm duct; 2) Urinary bladder and ureter; 3) Penis; 4) Accessory sex glands; a) Deferentio-vesical glands; b) Prostate gland; c) Bulb of urethra (after Dellmann, 1962).

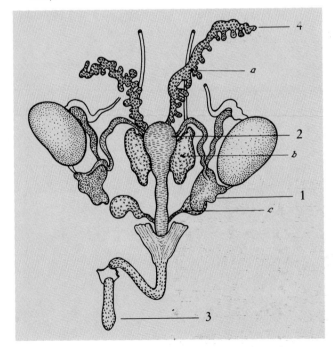

42

Arrangement of horny spines on copulatory organ: a) Lateral view; b) Underside; c) Upper side (Dellmann, 1962).

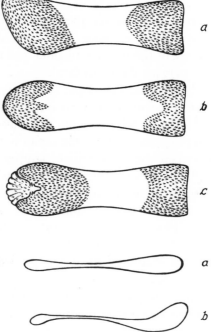

The baculum or supporting bone of the penis: a) Dorsal view; b) Lateral view (after Dellmann, 1962).

the urethra is slit-like over its final 3 cm or so and terminates — in contrast to that of many other mammals — outside the vagina. Labia are not present. In contrast to the buck, the female chinchilla has a very short perineum covered with fine hair.

## MALE SEX ORGANS

In male chinchillas the customary descent of the testes in the course of development from the kidney region into the scrotum is incomplete. The testes remain in the abdominal cavity and only the epididymis is located in an extrusion of the abdominal cavity. A scrotum does not occur in chinchillas. The testes, which weigh about 2.6 g and measure 2-2.5 by 1 cm, can even be smaller when situated deeper in the abdominal cavity without providing any conclusive indication in regard to their functionality. They push against the large intestine and the cecum, and they can also touch the urinary bladder. Leydig's interstitial cells, in contrast to other rodents, are poorly developed.

Lateral to the testis is the epididymis, where the sperm cells mature before they reach the sperm duct, which lead into the pelvic cavity. There the sperm ducts cross the mesentery of the urinary bladder and then open side-by-side into the urinary duct (urethra).

The copulatory organ (penis) is of an s-shape when in the resting position. It starts out from two supports at the lower side of the pelvic region. A short distance from where both supports have joints, the organ bends forward and downward between the intermediate support, finally pointing posteriorly again, with the glans penis terminating below the anus. The perineum is substantially longer in chinchilla bucks than in females. For the purpose of copulation the penis swells with blood flooding the cavernes and its tip erects forward. A club-shaped bone about 1 cm long serves as support. A special arrangement of backwardly pointing horny spines on the penis mechanically assures a better attachment during copulation. When at rest the foreskin extends up to the anus and its opening is relatively narrow.

The sex glands, which are arranged in three pairs (spermatocystic glands, prostate gland, Cowper's glands), have important functions during sperm transport. The thin-walled spermatocystic glands, with their strongly branched ducts 50-60 cm long and 1-3 cm thick, nearly fill out the entire pelvic cavity. They enter into the urethra jointly with the sperm ducts. They give off a yellowish gelatinous liquid that stimulates motility in sperm cells.

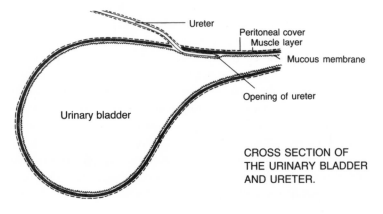

Ureter

Peritoneal cover
Muscle layer

Mucous membrane

Opening of ureter

Urinary bladder

CROSS SECTION OF
THE URINARY BLADDER
AND URETER.

44

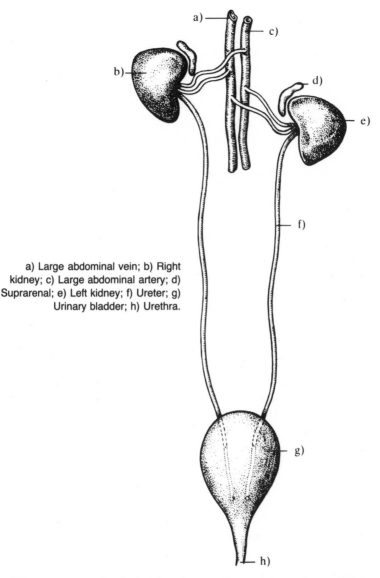

a) Large abdominal vein; b) Right kidney; c) Large abdominal artery; d) Suprarenal; e) Left kidney; f) Ureter; g) Urinary bladder; h) Urethra.

The prostate gland, in the shape of two triangular reddish brown lobes of 1-2 cm by 0.5 cm in size, is located laterally and above the urinary bladder and the proximal section of the urethra. It opens into the urethra somewhat in front of the sperm ducts. Its thin milky secretion serves primarily to dilute the sperm.

The Cowper's glands are two roundish, reddish brown

structures 0.5 cm in diameter. They are located below the root of the tail laterally to the rectum and behind the neck of the urinary bladder. Their ducts, externally fused but in reality strictly separated, enter the urethra from above. The function of their secretion serves to lubricate the penis during copulation. It has also been suggested that the secretion is to neutralize the urine present in the urethra and thus prepare the urethra for the passage of sperm.

A sexually fully mature, rested buck gives off about 0.1 to 0.2 ml of semen during each ejaculation, which contains approximately 120 million sperm cells. With two copulations observed per week there did not appear to be a reduction in sperm volume.

## URINARY APPARATUS

As in other mammals, the urinary apparatus in chinchillas consists of the kidneys, ureter, urinary bladder, and urethra. In adult animals the bean-shaped kidneys weigh about 1 g and are 18 x 13 x 5 mm. They are located to the left and right of the backbone along the upper abdominal wall in the region of the upper diaphragm; the right kidney is located slightly more forward than the left. At the opposite end (pole) of each kidney there is an elongated, dirty white to yellowish suprarenal gland, a hormonal gland of great importance for the regulation of organ functions. It displays a conspicuous dimorphism in size, shape, and weight. The suprarenal weight is somewhere between that of an albino rat and a guinea pig. The ureter exits at the navel-like indentation of the kidney (i.e., toward the middle of the body) and the blood and lymphatic vessels and the nerves enter at that point. The chinchilla kidney is of the so-called single-warted smooth type. The reniculi are fused and their original (rudimentary) primordium can only be recognized on the basis of the blood vessel arrangement.

The efferent urinary pathways start with the renal pelvis. The ureter (about 1 mm thick) enters here — separately for each side — into the urinary bladder just in front of its neck. When filled (only a few milliliters), the transparent bladder narrows backwardly toward the neck of the bladder. Both ureters enter at that point, as already mentioned, and the

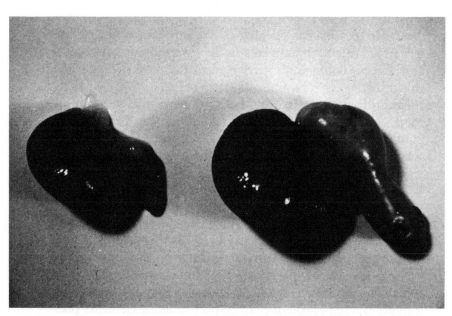

Kidneys and suprarenals from a chinchilla (suprarenals enlarged).

neck of the bladder from there changes into the urethra. Its anatomical pathway is determined by the sex of the individual.

### ANAL SAC

If one catches a chinchilla in its cage and holds on to it, one can observe in most cases how the anus opens intermittently and each time it does a bean-sized, yellow nodule becomes visible at the lower corner of the anal slit. At the same time one can detect a peculiar, strong odor. The opening of the anal sac is located inside of this yellow nodule.

The skunk is well-known for its ability to squirt the content of its anal sac to drive its enemies away. The unpleasant odor of this glandular secretion in skunks is only too well known. Dogs and cats also give off a pungent secretion from their anal sacs when these are full and the pet owner inadvertently presses against the anal region.

In the chinchilla the anal sac serves a similar function. Chinchillas can discharge odorous substances by deliberately

47

inverting the anal sac opening in the anus. According to observations this action appears to be a warning or fright reaction that no doubt is effective against the natural enemies of chinchillas.

According to reports from breeders these anal sacs can become chronically inflamed. This condition can be treated as in other animal species by flushing with astringents or glucocorticoid or sulfonamid solutions.

## ENDOCRINE ORGANS

The hypophysis display a ventro-caudally oriented infundibulum axis and a glandular body that is positioned nearly horizontally. A hypophysis cavity is always present. Using simple techniques one can recognize five chromophile cell types in the adenohypophysis. The abundance of pseudofollicles at the anterior lobe is conspicuous. *Recessus pinealis* has a single-layered ependyme. In respect to tissue elements present, the pineal body is more similiar to the epiphysis of horses than to that of other rodents.

An isthmus is only sometimes present at the thyroid gland.

Anal-genital region of a female; the anal sac is shown opened up.

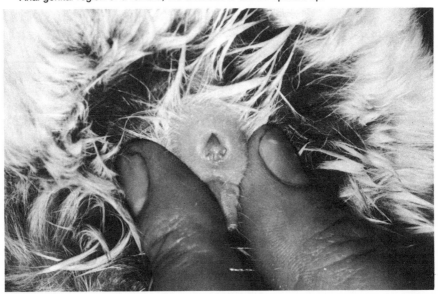

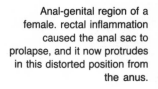
Anal-genital region of a female. rectal inflammation caused the anal sac to prolapse, and it now protrudes in this distorted position from the anus.

Displaying the colloidal pre-stages can be easily done by means of histological sections. C-cells occur interstitially, epifollicularly, and parafollicularly. Under toludene blue stain they show metachromatically reacting cytoplasm. Individual ganglia cells occur subcapsularly.

There are four epithelial bodies, two external and two internal. The parasympathic paraganglia are rich in ganglia cells. Those more toward the back of the *Paraganglion aorticum abdominale* and chromaffine (chromaphil) cells have become more predominant.

For suprarenals refer to urinary apparatus; for pancreas refer to digestive organs; for ovaries and testes refer to sex organs.

## SEASONAL DISEASE AND MORTALITY CYCLES

Intensive research in recent years on chinchilla husbandry problems has led to new findings that are of considerable

49

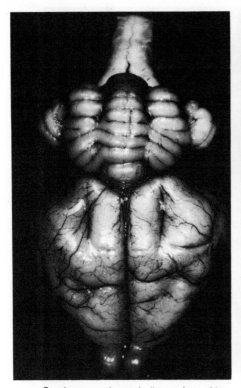 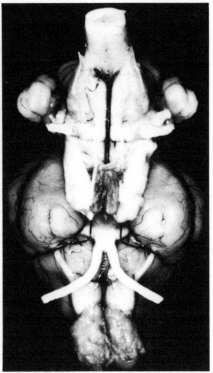

Cerebrum and cerebellum of a chinchilla. Dorsal view.

Cerebrum and cerebellum of a chinchilla. Ventral view.

benefit to all chinchilla breeders. One such problem has been
the common knowledge that incidences of disease and mortalities are higher during certain periods of the year than at
other times. A distribution curve prepared from veterinary
records clearly depicts an increase of autopsies during spring
(March and April) and again in autumn (September and October). Sex apparently does not have a significant influence
on the frequency of a particular disease, apart from sex-re-
lated disease (such as infections of the uterus and testes),
which, of course, can have a slight deviating affect on curve
progression.

Many more animals became ill during spring and fall than
at other times of the year, and consequently this increases
mortalities. A whole range of causes has been advanced for
this trend. First, there are weather changes that have a sud-

den effect on plants and animals. Here one has to keep in mind that the temperature increases in spring (temperature increases of 10-20°C can occur within a few days). Changes in diet also take place during this period: hay from the previous year's harvest is about used up, breeder feels he should give green food, etc.

Breeding rooms that have been heated during the winter are now being warmed by the sun only, and yet the sun never penetrates into many chinchilla breeding facilities directly for days on end or ever. This then means that the immediate surroundings, the walls, roof, or floor, have to be sufficiently warmed up in order to be able to actually ´'give off heat." This process takes at least two months until warmth radiates from the surroundings. This lag period can be monitored with a room thermometer and a hygrometer in order to find out what the "microclimate" is. During the winter months heaters of various types maintained the relative humidity at about 50%, but in spring it can suddenly rise to 70% from one day to the next. Chinchillas are extremely sensitive to sudden changes in microclimate. It is known, for instance,

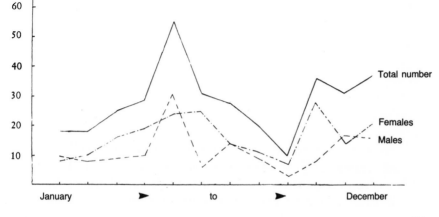

Autopsies performed on chinchillas, per month, during the years 1958 to 1961. The graphic representation clearly shows that there was a significant increase in mortalities during the months of April and September and a corresponding increase in disease cases. On the other hand, during the winter months January/-February and summer months July/August the rate of disease cases and of mortalities is lower. The peak of the number of autopsies performed is during spring, produced primarily by diseases of the gastrointestinal tract.

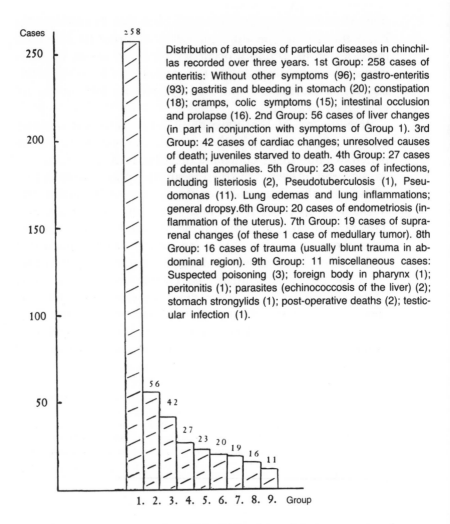

Cases

Distribution of autopsies of particular diseases in chinchillas recorded over three years. 1st Group: 258 cases of enteritis: Without other symptoms (96); gastro-enteritis (93); gastritis and bleeding in stomach (20); constipation (18); cramps, colic symptoms (15); intestinal occlusion and prolapse (16). 2nd Group: 56 cases of liver changes (in part in conjunction with symptoms of Group 1). 3rd Group: 42 cases of cardiac changes; unresolved causes of death; juveniles starved to death. 4th Group: 27 cases of dental anomalies. 5th Group: 23 cases of infections, including listeriosis (2), Pseudotuberculosis (1), Pseudomonas (11). Lung edemas and lung inflammations; general dropsy. 6th Group: 20 cases of endometriosis (inflammation of the uterus). 7th Group: 19 cases of suprarenal changes (of these 1 case of medullary tumor). 8th Group: 16 cases of trauma (usually blunt trauma in abdominal region). 9th Group: 11 miscellaneous cases: Suspected poisoning (3); foreign body in pharynx (1); peritonitis (1); parasites (echinococcosis of the liver) (2); stomach strongylids (1); post-operative deaths (2); testicular infection (1).

1. 2. 3. 4. 5. 6. 7. 8. 9. Group

that losses can occur after chinchillas have been transported only a short distance, even with the same food being given at points of origin and destination and under identical general environmental conditions.

Infections of stomach and intestine, colics, constipation, and intestinal occlusions are always caused by significant disturbances of intestinal flora. Certain bacteria normally present in stable ratios with many other bacteria suddenly increase dramatically or pathogenic bacteria are added. It is still a disputed question whether such single-celled organisms as amoebas or malaria-causing flagellates residing in the duodenum undergo a population explosion due to such disturbances and then become pathogenic or whether they can cause a specific primary disease. According to our observations, the organisms are present in the duodenum of chinchillas and they will only increase in numbers when there has been damage to the digestive tract. Therefore, dealing separately with this particular aspect of the large disease complex "infections of the digestive tract" is in my opinion superfluous.

During the critical period (March/April and September/October) the incidence of digestive tract diseases is higher than normal. Consequently, mortalities are higher than, for instance, death due to injuries (trauma). Yet it is also possible, for instance, to find an increase in uterine infections during these critical periods. Here it must be pointed out that apart from *Escherichia coli*, another organism also found in many digestive tract diseases is *Pseudomonas aeruginosa*. This organism spreads rapidly through the body and has also been implicated directly in uterine infections. The susceptibility to other infections such as listeriosis is also increased due to an incorrect diet and poor husbandry methods. Consequently, when reviewing a particular clinical picture the overall conditions of the facility must also be taken into consideration.

There is a significant increase in death during the months of April and September, with a corresponding increase in disease incidence. Yet during the winter months, January/February, and during the summer months, July/August, the disease and death rates are lower. The curve peaks in spring, made up primarily of chinchillas with diseases of the gastrointestinal system.

## HOW TO EXAMINE CHINCHILLAS

It is important to make sure that all disease manifestations are indeed detected during a comprehensive examination, so it is best to proceed with this along a predetermined, fixed routine. Since our chinchillas are somewhat different from the more common animal species encountered by most veterinarians, the following is a suggestion for such an examination routine.

The first step is a comprehensive *external* examination to

53

check for any superficial damage, injury, and/or other tissue changes on the animal's body, to recognize any locomotory (movement) disabilities, and to check for other obvious external symptoms. Identification symbols such as tattoos and ear marks must be recorded, as well as age and sex. The behavior of the animal during this preliminary examination is of considerable significance for later assessment. Experience has shown that chinchillas that can be easily caught by a stranger and which then sit quietly on his arm or hand are usually sick. Only hand-raised animals will ever behave this way even when healthy. The appearance and expression of the eyes often provide important clues about possible local or general diseases. Attention must also be paid to the feeding behavior and to the condition of the feces.

A close examination of the *oral cavity* is also very important. There we can recognize any dental problems and possibly remove any foreign body that could be fatal to the animal. Since the narrow mouth opening of chinchillas (in fact, all rodents) does not permit easy visual access, a special method has been developed. An otoscope, as used in human medicine for outer ear examinations, is inserted into a corner of the mouth alongside the incisor teeth. The first structures that come into view are the anterior areas of the molars. Through minor lateral movements one can illuminate and view the entire oral cavity up to the posterior wall of the trachea.

For this part of the examination the animal is restrained by its tail and supported on the lower arm. With the other hand one grasps both ears. Only in rare instances will the one who inserts the otoscope also have to restrain the front legs of the animal with his free hand. There is yet another way — wrap the animal in a towel, take it in one hand, and insert the otoscope as described above.

This same instrument can, of course, also be used for examining the *outer ear passage* in chinchillas.

Listening at the thoracic cavity will reveal to the trained examiner *heart* and *lung* irregularities.

Palpating (feeling) the *abdomen* is important when there is a suspicion of constipation or tumors. This method can also be used for diagnosing pregnancies.

54

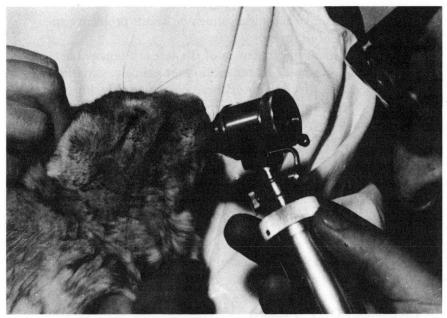
Examination of the oral cavity using an otoscope.

Examining the *body openings* (mouth, nose, anus, and sex openings) is also of importance. Here the color, increase in size, and any abnormal fluid discharge are significant indications of pathogenic processes.

Finally, an assessment of feces and urine in respect to color, volume, consistency, and odor is of particular importance. This permits conclusions about the correct functioning of the digestive process or any systemic malfunctions in this area.

This kind of general examination in chinchillas is generally followed by only a few specialized examinations such as pregnancy and x-ray tests. Should particular suspicions merit it, the body temperature can also be taken for three minutes with an ordinary rectal thermometer. A temperature measurement in chinchillas is usually not part of a general examination, since handling will upset the animals, which then tends to give an incorrect temperature reading. Unfortunately, examination possibilities are severely limited by the small size of the animals, but the examination routine suggested here can give early indications of health problems imminent or already present.

Examinations of the functions of the sensory organs refers to eyes, ears, and nose. As for most other animals, determining the flawless functioning of these organs in chinchillas is not easy because they cannot tell us whether they can see, hear or smell correctly. Therefore, the skilled examiner has to rely on reactions related to these organs. For instance, testing for correct visual ability is done through movements in front of the eyes without touching the animal. If the animal responds with proper eye movements it is presumed that the animal can see correctly. A similar method is used for testing the hearing in chinchillas, where directional movements of the ears are indicative of proper auditory ability. The sense of smell can be tested with strongly scented substances, such as ammonia or camphor.

## LABORATORY TESTS

Many laboratory tests require large amounts of test material that are difficult to obtain from animals as small as chinchillas, so there are definite limitations in this respect. Nevertheless, the most important tests (blood and urine analysis) can be performed.

*Blood* can be obtained by pricking the ear vein. By doing this repeatedly one can get a sufficient volume of blood for examination. Hematocrit, counting red and white blood cells, hemoglobin content, smears, and micro-depression tests can easily be done. Chinchillas have a high erythrocyte count and a lymphocytic blood picture.

Modern test strip methods for the determination of blood sugar, urine in blood, and hemoglobin can also be used for chinchillas. This requires merely a drop of blood. In fact, these test strip methods are indispensable for small husbandry. The accuracy of the strips fully conforms to the requirements of modern medicine, so they are indeed a valuable aid in diagnostics.

Similar methods have proven to be effective for the determination of alkaline and acid phosphates in blood. They are applicable to chinchillas since they also require only minor amounts of testing material (a few drops). It does not require

56

laboratory equipment and the tests are done in vials supplied with the kit.

A *urine analysis* is also readily done since 1-2 ml of urine are readily obtained from an animal. Commercially available test strips and tablets are used to check urine for protein content, bile stain, sugar, blood, and acetone (ketones). The rest of the urine sample can be used for testing sediments. Chinchilla urine has a composition typical for herbivorous animals. Pathological changes can easily be determined by above methods.

Finally, *parasitological and bacteriological fecal examinations* must be discussed. For these tests we use the same criteria as for other animal species, but it must be pointed out here that there are rarely any endoparasites in chinchillas apart from odd infestations of single-celled organisms (amoeba, etc.).

*Bacteriological examinations* of infected material is also done within the criteria applicable to other animals, but a few words need to be said about laboratory diagnostics of *fungus infections*. If there is — on the basis of hair loss — any suspicion of dermatomycosis (fungus infection of the skin), a few hairs (including their roots) are pulled out from along the edge of the visible pathological change. These hairs are then placed on a special nutrient medium (Sabouraud agar) and incubated at room temperature. If the animal indeed suffers from a fungus infection and the sample has been taken correctly, fungus will start to grow on the nutrient medium within a week. A microscopic examination will then identify the fungus species. This is the only way to correctly identify this rather specific type of disease and initiate an effective treatment.

# 4) Reproduction

## ESTRUS ("heat")

The fertility of an animal depends on many factors. It can be said that under favorable conditions chinchilla females can give birth to one to three (rarely four) young twice a year. Estrus, the so-called "heat," occurs for the first time in females when they are three to four months old. In *Chinchilla lanigera* the gestation period lasts for 111 days; in *Chinchilla brevicaudata* it lasts for 128 days. If a female does not conceive she will come back into "heat" every 28 to 35 days. Since a female can conceive again shortly after having given birth, there can theoretically be a birth three times a year. These are only theories, though, which rarely ever happen in reality.

The functional condition of a female's ovaries determines whether she comes into estrus or not. This in turn is dependent upon the general condition of the entire body system. Nutrition and maintenance play a very important role here. On the other hand, some hereditary traits are also decisive. I know of chinchilla groups where several females have never been "in heat" although they have been repeatedly paired off with different males, the diet was changed, and specific medication had been given.

A female in estrus can be recognized by her behavior and that of the buck. Although these animals are largely nocturnal so that their activities are not too often seen, the devastated appearance of the cage next morning will be conspicuous. Moreover, torn out fluffs of fur are also a sure sign.

Many authors and breeders report that the "heat plug" is a sure sign that a female has come into estrus. Up to now there has been no accurate, reliable information as to why and when this structure is secreted by chinchillas. In my experience, the plug does not appear with every estrus, apart from the fact that the usually dried up plug is easily overlooked. But I am certain that finding a heat plug (or whatever it is called) has no particular diagnostic sigificance, and neither does the absence of it indicate that estrus has not occurred. The only reliable sign that a female has come into estrus is the open vagina and the behavior of both partners. It must be remembered, though, that the vagina also remains open for a certain period after parturition (after having given birth). Moreover, this also applies to spontaneous abortions, which may have gone unnoticed. Also the vagina is commonly open when a female has a uterine disease problem, though there is then invariably a more or less copious vaginal discharge.

But now back to the topic of fertility in chinchillas. Following copulation and if a female has conceived, she can carry one or more young and then give normal birth to these in due course. It has also been observed that a female can give birth to one live and one dead young each. If three or even four young are born to the same female, one or more of these may not be viable. A nutritious, vitamin-rich diet supports the well-being of our animals and promotes proper body functions. We have to give a performance diet when we expect performance. Good breeding results are never achievable with a fattening diet or a mere maintenance diet. If there are no detrimental hereditary influences on the sex organs, vitamin E, mineral additives, and other dietary supplements will revitalize and support body functions.

Sometimes the question arises whether a chinchilla female has already been pregnant and/or whether she has previously given birth. The simplest way to find the answer would be to extract the relevant data from the respective pedigree certificate. Regrettably, this is not always possible. If animals like this are taken to a veterinarian he can determine from the condition of the vagina and the teats and from the age of the animal whether it has already been pregnant or given birth. However, an unequivocal result can only be obtained through an autopsy, specifically a histological examination of

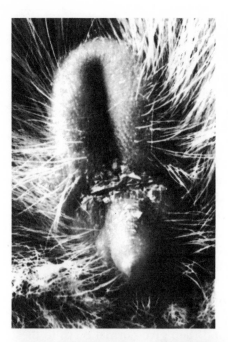

**Left:** External sex organs of female *Chinchilla lanigera*. Adjacent to the anus is the horizontal vagina (closed) and below that is the urethral uvula. **Below:** Various vaginal plugs. Top: copulatory plug; below: estral plug.

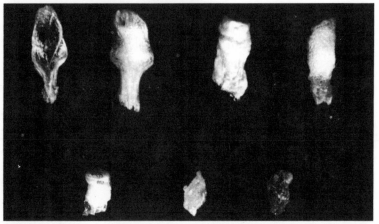

the sex organs. The ovaries, oviducts, and uterus must be examined so that the size of the sex organs, asymmetry of the uterine horns and a thickening of the uterine wall can provide relevant information. A histological examination of the uterine wall could possibly provide evidence of earlier pregnancies based on a determination of pigment deposits or a profusion of elastic tissue. Changes in the wall of the uterus and histological examinations of the ovaries are of considerable significance, since the uterus never quite regains its former shape following the first pregnancy.

## FERTILITY PROBLEMS IN CHINCHILLA FEMALES

The fertility of the animals is of fundamental importance for a successful chinchilla breeding facility. The cause for insufficient progeny can lie either with the females or with the buck and can manifest itself as temporary or permanent sterility. An exact diagnosis is absolutely essential before an effective treatment can be initiated.

Apart from poor maintenance, an inadequate diet, incorrect mating, or the presence of pathological conditions, the following causes of sterility prevail in females:

—inflammations and infections of sex organs, characterized by vaginitis, endometriosis, or pyometra;

—atrophy of ovaries, together with hormonal imbalance;

—general infection, such as *Pseudomonas aeruginosa*, which can affect the digestive tract as well as the sex organs.

Uterus of pregnant female. Left uterine horn with two embryos that had died after about two weeks, right uterine horn with embryo about seven weeks old.

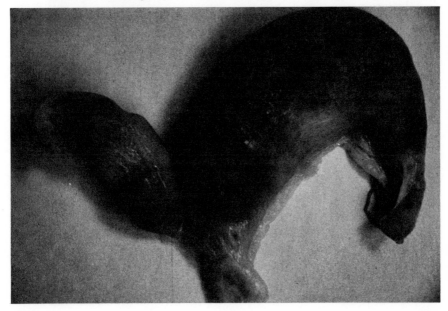

Abdominal cavity (open) of *Chinchilla lanigera*; intestine removed. Ovaries can be seen to the right of the kidneys; the inflamed, enlarged womb extends from the ovaries backward.

Inflammations and infectious processes of the female sex organs are characterized externally by encrustations around the open vagina (which is normally closed). A detailed inspection of the vaginal mucous membrane with an otoscope or a speculum may show this to be discolored dirty red. In cases of endometriosis and pyometra the mouth of the womb, normally arranged in duplicate, is open and has a purulent, slimy discharge. A bacteriological test often indicates the presence of *Pseudomonas aeruginosa*.

The cause of many of these infectious diseases often is dead embryos giving rise to subsequent infections of the uterus. Furthermore, in polygamous breeding there is often a transfer of pathogen(s) via the buck to other females. Such transmission of a disease from initially a single female to the entire polygamous breeding group can occur within two to three weeks. Effective treatment to save the entire stock requires isolation of all animals, including the buck.

General infections with *Pseudomonas aeruginosa*, which can

affect the digestive tract as well as the sex organs, are included in the causes of infectious diseases.

In 41 females that were alleged to be infertile, one worker found the following conditions:

—extended estrus period and reduced estrus cycle interval;

—extended estrus period and extended estrus cycle interval;

—not in estrus during copulation.

Histological examinations of the ovaries did not provide a typical diagnosis, but there were signs of degeneration on the

External sex organs of male *Chinchilla lanigera*. Please note the distinct spacial separation between anus and penis.

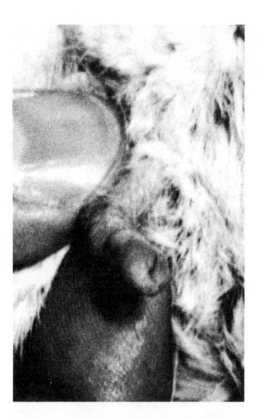

Penis.

suprarenals. The estrus cycle could have been modified with cortiocosteroids or corticosteroids plus serumgonadotropin respectively (but not the ability to conceive).

Sulfonamides and antibiotics are recommended for the treatment of infectious diseases; ideally, each treatment should be preceded by a determination of the relevant antibiotic resistance.

Hormonal disorders of the ovaries are of considerable importance, but the underlying causes have not yet been determined. Treatment of hormonal problems is done in accordance with established procedures for other animal species.

## MALE FERTILITY AND ABILITY TO COPULATE

Success in chinchilla breeding is dependent not only upon female fertility, but also upon the fertility of the male and its ability to copulate. There is heavy pressure on males in polygamous breeding groups, and only those animals that are healthy and active can produce flawless progeny. An assessment of a newly acquired buck in respect of its fertility is not easy, and usually the breeder will have to rely on an initial trial.

The externally visible genitalia of a chinchilla buck must, of course, be without any genetic, morphological, or pathological problems. The testes can be felt when palpating — with two fingers — the abdomen between the hind legs. Chinchillas, unlike most other mammals, do not have a scrotum; the testes and epididymis are located in an indentation of the abdominal musculature. I have, however, seen a number of bucks where the testes were located in the abdominal cavity and the indentation of the abdominal wall was absent. Research in this area has not yet shown whether this has any bearing on fertility. Histological studies on sperm formation in various mammals with testes in the abdominal cavity or in an indentation of the abdominal musculature do not yet permit any conclusions about fertility, since all testes studied contained sperm in various phases of development. It appears to be irrelevant whether the testes in a chinchilla buck are intra-abdominal or are located in an indentation in the abdominal musculature. Consequently, the fertility of chinchilla bucks can only be judged on the basis of numerous and healthy progeny, provided the females are fertile.

The ability to copulate is not necessarily always related to

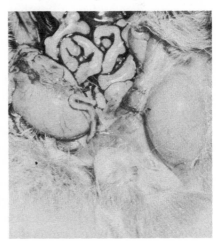

Testicles of fully grown buck *in situ*. The right testicle (in the picture) is still located in the indentation of the abdominal musculature ("testicle pouch"); only the skin is here removed. The left testicle is located inside the opened abdominal cavity and has been removed from the muscle indentation.

fertility. For instance, a chinchilla buck with a broken foot is temporarily unable to copulate, but it is still fertile. A fertile buck can also become temporarily unable to copulate due to exhaustion. Moreover, hair rings around the penis where the foreskin (prepuce) is pushed backward render many bucks unable to copulate. This is something every breeder has to watch for, and should hair rings occur they will have to be removed promptly.

*Penis prolapse* occur relatively often in chinchillas. This condition commonly appears to be due to nervous disturbances or irritability. It must be treated promptly or bites and other injuries can occur, possibly even necrosis, and the animal may have to be put down for humane reasons. Treatment consists of medication that reduces swelling and acts as a muscle relaxant. The penis may have to be coated with a mild ointment such such as penicillin eye ointment since it can relatively quickly dry out during prolonged prolapse. I have found the following therapeutic treatment to be very effective. First give an injection of a spasmolyticum; after a waiting period of 5 to 10 minutes the penis is gently dabbed with a mucous membrane topical anesthetic and then the already partially relaxed penis is pushed back under the foreskin. Some ointments can be applied under the prepuce.

A temporary separation of buck and female is advisable. The main causes of penis prolapse seem to be on one hand over-exhaustion as among polygamous bucks on a nutritionally poor diet and on the other over-exhaustion of nervous bucks that have been kept away from females. These conditions have to be taken into consideration separately from any medical treatment given.

Traumatically induced changes to the testes can occur, but this is hardly ever noticeable in live animals. Since chinchilla testes are not located in an externally visible scrotum but instead in a indentation of the abdominal musculature, any inflammation could only be recognized by a painful reaction during palpation.

An autopsy sometimes reveals changes of one or both testes. If these occur on one side only they may well have been caused by trauma. Explicit details can only be ascertained through a histological examination.

## ARTIFICIAL INSEMINATION

Artificial insemination (AI) is today a widely used method in animal production. Veterinary medicine has advanced this type of fertilization to such a degree that there are hardly any difficulties with the collection, dilution, and storage of sperm. The reasons for artificially inseminating animals are, among others:

—selection of genetically valuable material;
—better utilization of the ejaculate;
—to overcome copulating difficulties;
—isolation of epidemic diseases transmitted by copulation.

It is primarily a question of funding whether a breeder can afford to maintain a genetically valuable stud buck. This would be purely a luxury in small operations. Moreover, stud bucks with good qualities are always rarer than those with poor qualities. If a breeder wants to go into a special mutation the financial burden becomes even greater.

Another important point in favor of artificial insemination is the fact that during each copulation (under natural conditions) the ejaculate (the entire volume of semen is about .01 to .2 ml in chinchilla bucks) is given into the female's vagina. Yet only one or two spermatozoa (on the average) fertilize a corresponding number of eggs. The rest (about 120 million sperm in chinchillas) perish. Artificial insemination capitalizes on this generosity of nature, allowing the ejaculate to be diluted with special liquids, so one ejaculate can be used to fertilize several females.

Copulating difficulties are quite frequent in mammals. This can be due to incompatible sizes of the partners or for reasons of social hierarchy within a particular animal community, where the better male (in terms of the breeding objectives) is being forced away by a physically stronger but genetically inferior male. Finally, copulation can also become impossible because of genital anomalies due to previous injuries. In such cases artificial insemination can provide a valuable alternative.

Artificial insemination can also restrict the spread of communicable diseases by eliminating their transmissions via copulation. These are all points which are fundamentally valid for most mammal species, without considering specific peculiarities of certain species.

Artificial insemination in chinchillas was practiced some years ago in the United States, but it did not succeed. This could have been due to personal interests of individual breeders, but it also could have failed because of anatomical and functional peculiarities in chinchillas in that conception is not always assured in these animals by methods of artificial insemination.

Sperm collecting is fairly easy in chinchillas. Manual stimulation (stimulating the male with the fingers) as well as electric shock (stimulating the anal region with a low voltage electrode) have been tried and shown to provide sufficient semen. With the manual method, however, there is a danger of contaminating the ejaculate with urine. Also, a more rapid coagulation of the semen is possible due to oxygen access than with the electric shock method.

Freeze-drying and dissolution plus dilution of the ejaculate are done according to the same guidelines as for other mammal species. Selection of a buck is preceded by a close examination of its sperm for volume, motility, shape, and bacteria content. This process, however, requires special equipment and experience, so that only qualified establishments can supply viable sperm for artificial insemination.

The actual difficulty with artificial insemination starts with the transfer of the semen into the female. The dissolved semen, brought to the correct body temperature, now has to be passed into the genital tract of the female. Firstly, this tract is very narrow so that extremely narrow-gauge glass instruments are required; secondly, the female has to be in estrus. The latter can be determined either from externally visible characteristics such as an open vagina, expulsion of "heat plug," and the appropriate behavior, or purely by means of simple arithmetic. The best practice is using both methods.

Research has shown that three to four estrus periods occur at intervals of 37 + 5 days, followed by a longer interval without estrus. Our breeders usually talk about estrus cycles of mostly 28 days. The most successful inseminations in chinchillas are made 15 to 20 days after parturition. These are just guidelines because one would expect individual variations to occur, and the breeder simply has to recognize these and take them fully into consideration. Finally, it is also essential that there are follicle fractures in the ovaries — some eggs are being freed for fertilization and move into the oviduct — because only under these circumstances can artificial insemination be successful.

One more problem arises in chinchillas when artificial insemination is used. Due to the small size of the genital organs the semen cannot be injected directly into the uterus, as is done in cattle, which would lead to more reliable fertilization results. Instead, in chinchillas the semen has to be applied to the vagina and one has to hope that sufficient sperm find their way through the open mouth of the uterus — which in this species has a double structure in the form of a duplex uterus — toward the oviduct and so to the eggs that are to be fertilized. This anatomical obstacle tends to influence the success rate of artificial insemination in chinchillas. Nevertheless, the literature quotes a fertilization success of 60 to 70%, but this is not necessarily an indication of the number of actual progeny eventually born.

Obviously, artificial insemination in chinchillas can be of valuable assistance for particular breeding programs and under special circumstances. However, biological insemination (copulation) under monogamous and polygamous conditions remains the medium of choice.

Unfortunately, artificial fertilization of chinchillas did not take hold in the industry. The technical and biological problems apparently outweigh its usefulness. The two most important criteria for using artificial insemination — its more effective use of sperm volume and isolation of actually or potentially diseased stock — are irrelevant in chinchilla production. Moreover, the small size of the species turns sperm collecting into a delicate manipulation.

## PREGNANCY DIAGNOSIS
Veterinarians are constantly being asked to diagnosis chinchillas for possible pregnancies. Confirmation of pregnancies in mammals can come from various sources, including among other things an actually observed copulation. A veter-

inarian's investigative opportunities are limited with such a small animal as a chinchilla. Understandably, palpating the animal's abdominal region is really of value only during late-term pregnancy. If this is correctly done the embryo will not be injured and a spontaneous abortion due to mishandling is not likely, even though some people like to imply this! During the last weeks of pregnancy the embryos can be felt clearly. The enlarged mammary glands and teats are also an indication of the imminent end of a gestation period. An x-ray examination is only indicated in very doubtful cases, and it is only of significance toward the end of the gestation period. By then embryos have developed skeletal structures that show up on the film (the fur of animals that are x-rayed once or twice during their life will not be damaged by the rays). An externally visible increase in abdominal area or a weight increase is — by itself — not evidence of an existing pregnancy. Laboratory tests for pregnancy diagnosis in chinchillas have not yet been developed, and developing them would probably be difficult because of the small amount of study material available.

In summary, what can be said about pregnancy diagnosis in chinchillas is that a female can only be diagnosed as pregnant when the embryos can be clearly felt or they are visible on x-ray film. In all other cases one can only speak of a presumed pregnancy.

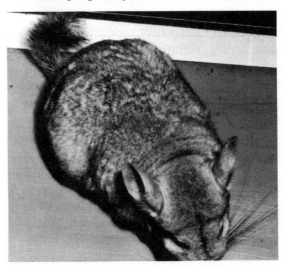

Pregnant female about four weeks prior to parturition.

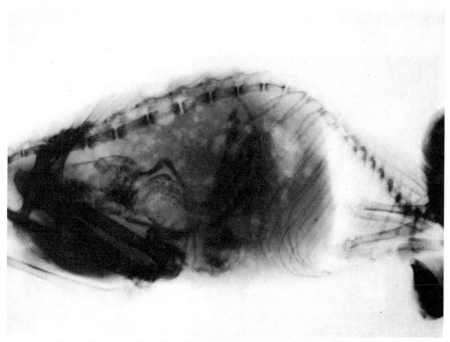
X-ray of pregnant female with near-term embryo in birth position.

The most conclusive evidence of pregnancy is a birth corresponding to an observed copulation. The gestation periods are then read off the littering calendar. One has to take into consideration, though, that chinchillas generally have gestation periods that can vary by one or two days. In such cases it is important to remember that "delayed" pregnancies can also be due to pathological changes. The animals must be closely monitored to determine whether it is a "normal delayed" pregnancy or whether a pathological condition has set in. If in doubt, contact a veterinarian.

## PARTURITION PROBLEMS
For a breeder it is often rather difficult to provide obstetric support because of the narrow birth pathway, although this may sometimes become necessary. Poor contractions, birth passages that are too narrow, or embryos that are too large cannot only delay parturition but sometimes even make parturition impossible. If an embryo becomes lodged in the vagina, one can attempt at the onset of contractions to gently

71

Newly born young; the mother is pulling out the next one.

free it through a downwardly directed, twisting pull. Poor contractions can be mediated with the same medications as used for other animals but with a suitably adjusted dosage.

## CAESAREAN SECTION

The following incident is described here as an example of veterinary intervention in a case of an animal encountering difficulties during parturition. A chinchilla female was taken to a veterinarian for a pregnancy examination. Palpation revealed that this female was in a late-term pregnancy. Fourteen days later this female displayed signs of minor contractions that did not seem to properly initiate parturition. A diagnosis of "onset of parturition with poor contractions" was made and the animal was given a subcutaneous injection of 0.1 ml Hypophysin. This enhanced contractions but did not effect parturition. By palpating the animal's abdominal region one could feel a relatively large embryo that had already moved into the pelvic cavity. Since the female had already become apathetic, a decision was made to perform a Caesarean section. Because of the female's poor overall condition it was deemed inadvisable to use a general anesthesia; instead, a local anesthetic was given (2% Isocain into the abdominal wall musculature and underneath the skin along the cutting line). An opening was cut into the left flank, as is commonly done in other animal species these days. The animal was held by its front and hind legs and did not offer any resistance during the operation.

Initially the cut was made only large enough for one finger to be inserted into the abdominal cavity. This revealed that the embryo, which was really too large (subsequent measurement indicated a length of 12 cm from top of head to base of

Caesarean section with opening of abdominal cavity.

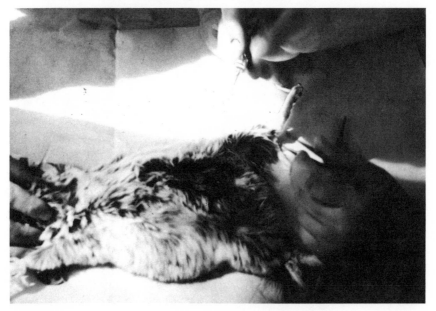

Obesity in chinchillas can cause problems in general health care and specifically in breeding programs.

Obviously a freshly dead chinchilla can be handled (for autopsy, etc.) differently from the way a live chinchilla would have to be handled.

tail), was already dead and out of the uterus into the abdominal cavity. An early stage of peritonitis suggested that the embryo must have broken through the womb some time earlier. Because of the hopeless condition of the female it was humanely put to sleep. The embryo had a complete coat and it gave the impression that it had been carried beyond full-term. The snout was strongly compressed and appeared to have been stuck in the entrance to the pelvic cavity of the female before the wall of the womb tore. Since the birth passage was simply too narrow for the enormously large embryo and the contractions kept on pushing it, the embryo was finally forced through the womb.

Now some general comments about Caesarean sections in chinchillas. From my own experience as well as from written and verbal communication of other colleagues, it can be said that in principle it is feasible. For anatomical reasons the cut should be made along the midline of the abdomen. General anesthesia presents absolutely no difficulties. Observing the usual precautionary measures, a 5% Thiogenal solution (80 mg/kg body weight) is injected into the abdominal cavity; other authors recommend 50 mg/kg. The animal goes under in about two to three minutes, has complete tolerance for about one to one and a half hours, and then sleeps for several hours. A female in poor condition should be given Ketanest (20 mg/kg) and a local anesthetic for the operation. Sometimes it may become necessary to remove the uterus, so the animal can no longer be used for breeding. The breeder has to give serious consideration in terms of his breeding objectives and for reasons of animal welfare as to whether an animal that has had a Caesarean section should be used for further breeding.

# 5) The Young

It need not be unduly stressed that having the natural mother rear her own young is by far the best rearing method. If there are no *birth defects* or *lack of milk in the mother*, every effort should be made to keep the young with their mother. In nearly all cases the buck, in a polygamous breeding group, can then also retain free access. Rarely will he ever need to be locked up separately. Even young from the previous litter that are still in the same group do not present any problems. Here, however, the overall situation in the entire group will have to be carefully considered. If the animals are frequently disturbed, that is, if there is too much noise around the colony or if the animals are removed too often from the cage, all this can lead to anxiety in nursing mothers. This in turn may

The two right teats of a nursing chinchilla female.

cause injury to the young or the female may even kill her own young.

## REARING PROBLEMS

As long as the litter consists of only one or two young there is hardly ever a problem. Yet, if the female has given birth to three or even four young she can suffer from a lack of milk. It is also possible that there is not enough space in the cage, which can lead to injuries or even fatalities. In any event, even a high-energy diet and adequate liquid for the mother will not solve such problems. Instead, direct action is generally required. Three different approaches can be used to tackle these problems.

Firstly, the young can be given supplementary feedings, with the weaker ones offered once or twice a day a fixed amount of milk, initially from a pipette and later on from a small bottle. It is important to make sure that the milk intended for the young is not taken by the mother or the buck instead.

Secondly, one or two of the strongest young can be separated from the mother during one meal each day in order to give the weakest an opportunity to get their fill and also to afford the mother some rest from the constant attempts of

Newborn chinchilla, already dry, attempting to walk.

Three-day-old young *Chinchilla brevicaudata* weighing 85 g.

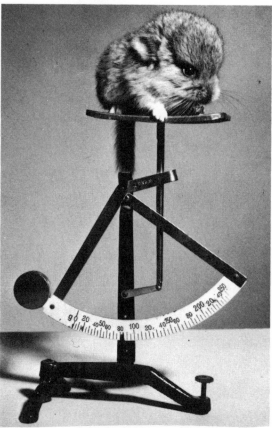

Motherless young being bottle-fed.

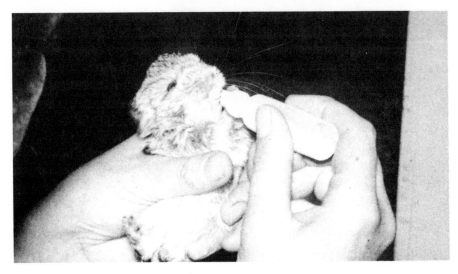

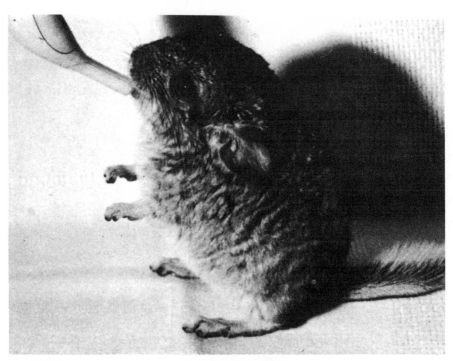
Soon the young drinks from a bottle without being held.

such a large number of young to gain access to her teats. Nevertheless, in most cases it will become necessary to provide supplementary feedings for the separated young.

As a third possibility, one or two of the young can be removed from the mother for artificial rearing. It is rarely possible to give these young to a foster mother, since a suitable female is usually not available when needed. Moreover, females usually do not accept the young from others.

## ARTIFICIAL REARING

Rearing young chinchillas artificially does not present any significant difficulties. It is important, however, that the newborn receives some *colostral milk (colostrum)* during the first few hours of its life. This is the very first mother's milk, and it contains the required antibodies commonly passed on from the female to her young. This tends to build up immunity against infectious diseases during the first few weeks. If this does not take place (such as if the mother dies during parturition or she does not have any milk at all) the young is seriously endangered. In such an event attempts should be made to establish immunity artificially with non-specific stimulus therapy such as gamma globulin.

The artificial rearing diet formula can easily be mixed and administered. It consists of diluted condensed milk — one part unsweetened condensed milk and two parts boiled water. This mixture is given via a pipette (sterilized through boiling) at two-hour intervals (also at night!). Newly born chinchillas readily take to this form of feeding, but it is important to make sure that the animals do not drink too fast, which could cause choking followed by loss of consciousness. (This usually does not require any intervention since the ani-

Young chinchillas; on the right are three-day-old young; the animals at left are three weeks old.

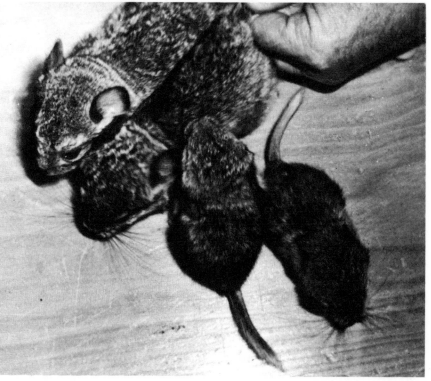

mals invariably recover within a few seconds.) Care must be taken that the milk mixture is given at body temperature, and it must not be permitted to turn sour. One should not attempt to keep a supply of it in a water bath for the next feeding, but instead always prepare it fresh. Strangely, all animals so far reared artificially have always shown preferences for particular brands of condensed milk. Experimentation is called for.

Invariably the chinchillas quickly learn to drink from a bottle, which after a brief adjustment period can simply be suspended inside the cage. It is important to give only enough formula for one feeding.

During the first few days the young drink about 15 ml, then 30 to 40 ml of diluted milk. After a week a larger amount can be given in the evening, which provides sufficient food for the animal until early the next morning. Soon thereafter the young can also be given some crisp wheat crackers such as zwieback, melba toast, or bread sticks with the salt grains scraped off.

From the third week one should offer a few strands of high quality hay and some partially crushed pellets. After the fourth week the milk mixture need to be given only three times a day, and additional liquid is then supplied with water from a regular drinking bottle. Right from the start the young chinchillas should be kept in a cage since they are quite capable of climbing and jumping. There must be a hiding place with soft bedding in the cage, and, depending upon the ambient temperature, it may have to be heated for the first six to ten weeks. This is essentially a substitute for maternal body heat.

In order to assure proper nutrition for rearing there must be two types of monitoring — of the feces and of the weight. Usually the weight increase levels off at the beginning of the second week, but at the end of the second week the weight has doubled and at the end of the third week it has tripled. After eight to ten weeks the young should weigh about 200 g (initial weight at birth is about 40 to 45 g).

The artificial diet must include vitamins, such as twice weekly supplements of a multi-vitamin compound. If there are any digestive problems they usually occur when there is a dietary change from milk to solid food (initially after the first week and then again somewhere around the sixth to eighth week). Problems usually manifest themselves as soft feces and a reluctance to feed. Should this happen it is advisable to strongly dilute the milk (1:4), offer chamomile tea, and give sulfonamide orally. If recognized and treated in time, feces consistency usually returns to normal the next day, the animal feeds properly again, and the danger is over.

If these guidelines are carefully complied with and the animal is watched there can be much pleasure in artificially rearing young chinchillas. Because of this close, constant contact the animals tend to become permanently imprinted upon humans and will remain hand-tame.

## ACCIDENTS

Accidents can happen when young are being reared, so it is important to pay special attention to a few major points. If the young are staying in the cage with their parent it is advisable to either remove the bottom wire for a few weeks or at least secure it firmly. The mesh width must be sufficiently narrow so that the young cannot get their toes caught in the wire. If the bottom grate is not secured adequately it can happen that the young chinchillas dislodge it while running around in the cage, so gaps could occur between the wire and the cage wall or bottom tray and the small animals could become wedged there. If there is no accurate daily monitoring (all animals must be counted!) such a trapped animal can easily be overlooked, particularly when stuck along the back wall.

There are dangers in store for animals that are being reared artificially and given free run in a room or apartment. They may gnaw on electrical wiring or slip off plastic furniture. Young chinchillas are extremely agile from early life on and will only hurt themselves when they fall onto concrete or tile floors.

## JUVENILE MORTALITY

One of the main operational objectives in animal production is to achieve the highest possible rate of reproduction together with the lowest mortality rates. This is particularly important when young are being reared. Qualified and experienced breeders usually have juvenile mortalities that are below 10%. This demonstrates clearly that losses can occur in spite of the best possible care. The main causes of juvenile mortalities are:

—death shortly before, during or after birth;
—deformities;
—an absolute or relative lack of milk in nursing females;
—change of diet from milk to solid food at an age of one week or six to eight weeks, respectively;
—infections and accidents.

The fundamental requirements for successful rearing are optimal care and nutrition for pregnant or nursing females and their young. The animals must not be "fattened," so they should not get protein-rich concentrated foods, but at the same time nutritional deficiencies must be avoided. Particularly critical is the supply of vitamins and minerals. Specific consideration must be given to the following:

First and foremost in importance is the proper care and monitoring of pregnant females. The litter date must be known and the pregnancy should be monitored through regular weight checks. (Some breeders feel that excessive handling of pregnant females, as in weight checks, may cause abortions, but opinion on this is divided.) This facilitates early recognition of premature births, stillbirths, resorption of embryos, and mummification of embryos.

With an approaching birth the cage must be lined with clean paper so that possible traces of blood can be spotted quickly. This would indicate injuries to the female or her young during parturition and confirm the passing of the afterbirth. The absence of dark red spots after parturition could be an indication of retention of the afterbirth.

Dead or mummified embryos develop through incorrect or insufficient nutrition. Resorption of embryos during early developmental stages is due to the same reasons or because of stress situations such as accidents or noise pollution.

There also are, of course, genetic influences that can lead to non-viable young at birth. Yet, not all young that are weak at birth should be automatically written off! Frequently all it takes for the animal to recover is removing parts of the afterbirth or mucus from the nose and mouth of the young or giving gentle artificial respiration.

While the comments made so far referred to the first few hours after parturition, an absolute or relative lack of milk in nursing females often does not become apparent for one or two days. The young are restless and they fight for a place at one of the female's nipples. This often leads to injuries to the female. The worst situation is an absolute lack of milk; that is, the female has no milk at all regardless of the number of young because her hormonal system is not functioning properly. This problem can often be overcome during the first two days with an Orastin injection (0.2 ml).

If the female has given birth to more than two young she may not have enough milk for all the young, which then leads to a relative lack of milk.

Losses due to a change in diet occur initially at an age of one week. Although the young are still nursing, they also begin to feed on some of the solid food given to the adults. It is important to make sure that the young do not have access to food that is too concentrated or to dietary supplements that could be damaging to the digestive tract of the young, which is still adjusted to a milk diet.

At an age of about six weeks (at a weight of approximately 200 g), when the young are being weaned, there is the possibility of disease if the dietary change-over is done too quickly. The best way to avoid this problem is by giving small rations of hay, which requires a lot of slow chewing.

**DEFORMITIES**

Deformities occur among all animals, and so it may be interesting to find out what deformities have so far been observed in chinchilla breeding. First of all, we have to distinguish between deformities that are due to cellular changes during embryonic development (genetic) and those caused by an outside source during parturition and development (traumatic or congenital).

Embryonic development progresses according to a predetermined natural scheme. For instance, during the first few

Siamese twins form a litter of quadruplets. Two completely developed females, pulled apart. They are fused from along the base of the neck to the navel region; two heads, four pairs of legs, and two tails.

weeks the rudimentary extremities are being developed. If a disorder occurs during any stage of the development, this can well lead to deformities.

Here, for instance, it may be relevant to relate to the reader the reports from two practicing veterinarians, each about the "birth" of an embryo "monster" known as a *schistosoma reflexum*. This involves a non-viable, usually full-term embryo where at a certain embryonic stage the two lower body halves did not grow together so that the abdominal organs are not enclosed. The birth of such a deformed embryo can often be recognized early when, following contractions, sections of intestine protrude from the female's vagina. These are usually the intestinal parts of a *schistosoma reflexum* that has become wedged by the contractions perpendicularly in front of the exit of the birth passage. Only the free, unenclosed organs are then pushed through the vagina because of their greater mobility. A dead embryo can usually only be removed by Caesarean section.

Another commonly observed deformity in chinchillas is Siamese twins. These are twins from a single fertilized egg

86

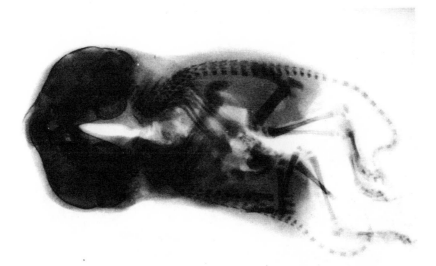

**Above:** X-ray of Siamese twins. The duplicate sets of bones are clearly visible. **Below:** All organs in the Siamese twins are in duplicate in a mutual chest and abdominal cavity.

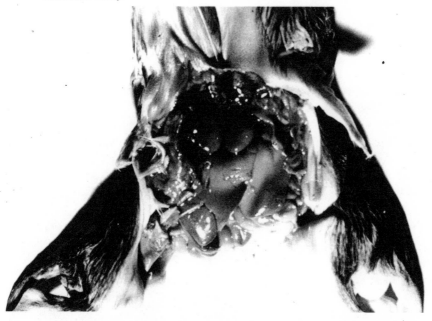

(therefore of the same sex and identical stage of development) where usually all the body parts and organs are arranged in duplicate but the two bodies have not become completely separated. For instance, the two bodies may remain fused

87

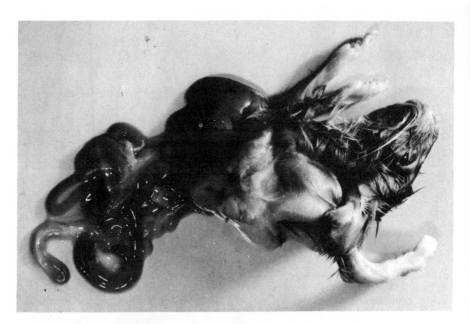

**Above:** *Schistosoma reflexum* removed by Caesarean. **Below:** *Schistosoma reflexum* of *Chinchilla lanigera*. The hind legs have been bent forward across the back to their maximum extent. The exposed organs are shown (full-term embryo).

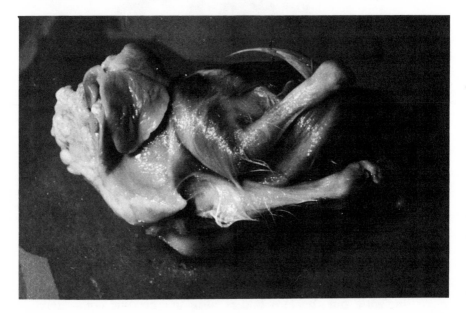

from the beginning of the neck to the navel region. Young that are deformed in this manner usually live only a short time. In contrast to the earlier mentioned deformity, the birth of this particular deformity is usually no more complicated than the one of an embryo that is too large, normally requiring only minimal outside help in order to bring this extraordinary embryo to the light of day. Frequently the breeder or consulting veterinarian become confused by the fact that at the onset of parturition there are possibly two tails or three legs and two tails appearing simultaneously in the birth passage. Fundamentally, the most effective support that can be given in a case like this is presence of mind and calm actions.

Apart from such extreme deformities there are also minor oddities, especially in the protruding extremities of the embryo. Consequently, the feet, ears, and tail can be developed incompletely and so lead to crippled appendages. Such deformities are not infrequently found in chinchillas. They can be due to disturbances during embryonic development or caused by incorrect actions of the mother or the breeder during parturition. If an embryo becomes wedged in the birth passage and part of it is already protruding from the vagina, the female will often attempt to pull it out. Often the breeder may attempt the same. This is absolutely wrong! If a pregnant female is in obvious difficulties help must be provided, but this must be done calmly and with sound reasoning. On one hand, attempts must be made to prevent the female from injuring the young with her sharp gnawing teeth, but the breeder must never try to help by pulling on a protruding foot, ear, or tail to free the young. The danger of injuring the young is too great! Since chinchilla tissue regenerates easily, thus initially healing any wounds, the breeder has produced an "artificial" deformity. Only with a "twisting pull" and by grasping as much as possible of the young's body and body parts can the wedged embryo possibly be freed. Frequently a Caesarean section is the only way to save the female; the young suffocates when it remains for too long in the birth tract of the female.

Once I saw a chinchilla that had a shortened lower jaw so that the gnawing teeth were in incorrectly opposing positions and they would not grind down properly. This then required frequent filing down of the gnawing teeth together with a special diet of soft food to keep the otherwise quite active animal alive. Here it must be pointed out that this condition is unrelated to true dental anomalies.

"Artificially" induced deformities due to traumatic injuries during the birth process do not have any influence on future progeny. Other deformities, however, incurred during the embryonic development deserve our undivided attention. Females that frequently produce young with deformities must be excluded from further breeding.

# 6) Physical Disorders

## FRACTURES

Chinchillas are naturally active animals that can sustain all sorts of injuries. Various wounds and bone fractures with all the inherent complications such as inflammations and blood poisoning (septicemia) are known to occur in chinchillas. Treating these is done in essentially the same way as in other animals: clean wound dressing; ointments to support healing of simple wounds; antibiotics or sulfonamides for inflammations. Abscesses are lanced and treated with the required disinfecting or bactericidal medications. Dressings are invariably difficult to apply and it is therefore recommended that the animal be given a neck collar to prevent it from gnawing or licking its wounds. Here one must never underestimate the agility of chinchillas — there are practically no parts of the body that they cannot reach with their snouts or their paws.

Fractures will have to be attended to in such a way that infections from simultaneous wounds are inhibited. Beyond that, attempts should be made to secure a cast or rigid bandage over the fractures so that both ends are held in place to heal properly. Here it has to be remembered that chinchillas sit on their hind legs when feeding, and food is generally held in the front paws. Consequently, with fractures there can be, one way or the other, subsequent feeding problems. A cast can inhibit proper feeding and the animal will have to be fed artificially. Generally fractures are not difficult to recognize: the distal end usually hangs loosely and the limb is not used. Often an amputation is the only solution, and many animals have shown that chinchillas are quite capable of leading a virtually normal life on only three limbs.

An unusual accident! While playing around in its cage a Lanigera female got its tail caught in the cage door. When the female ran away the bushy tip of the tail got torn off, and simultaneously the two upper tail tendons were pulled out along their entire length (12 cm). The wound healed completely and tail position remained as it was before the accident.

The following wound treatment medications have proven to be highly effective in promoting healing: cod liver ointment, hydrogen peroxide, chamomile tea, Rivanol solution (all solutions diluted as required), iodine tincture, antibiotic ointments, sulfonamide ointments, and antibiotic-sulfonimide ointments. There are many more, but the selection listed here provides adequate medication for proper treatment of the injuries discussed above. It need not be stressed that if a general infection due to an injury is suspected the reader should refer to the details in the chapter on infectious diseases.

In the event of major injuries or fractures the breeder is advised not to try out "home remedies" but to instead seek veterinary care. A detailed professional examination in conjunction with an x-ray, if need be, will provide explicit diagnosis so the correct treatment can be initiated.

**BITES**

When the animals have bite wounds, the breeder must determine whether there are possible incompatibilities among some of the cage occupants or if one of the females in a polygamous group has managed to get rid of the collar and ventured into her neighbor's cage. The latter invariably leads to serious fighting. But it can also happen that the buck is not welcomed by certain females in some of the cages, and again there will be fighting. This is particularly common among newly paired animals where the two animals simply "cannot stand the sight of each other."

## CONVULSIONS

It is not too uncommon to hear from veterinarians about convulsions in chinchillas, though actual observations come primarily from those who keep the animals since this sort of disorder occurs only spasmodically and then lasts for only a few seconds or minutes at the most. Treatment is dependent upon the cause of such convulsions, and there are many possibilities:

—causes initiated directly (primarily) by the brain, such as hemorrhaging due to accidents or tumors;

—causes due to various types of deficiencies such as calcium, vitamins, and certain minerals;

—injuries of the nervous system (brain, spinal cord, and primary afferent nerves);

Abscess between penis and anus about 2.5 cm in diameter.

—cardiac damage and circulatory disorders;
—infections.

All these symptoms can also occur as peripheral manifestations of other diseases, such as cardiac damage due to excessive stress and similar disorders. Convulsions are often observed following copulation and are then obviously related to the circulatory system. Here it must be pointed out that in chinchillas none of these disorders can be diagnosed directly, and therefore we have to initiate an empirical (experience-based) treatment.

It is now apparent that the best medication for all "convulsions" or "spasms" is to leave the animals in peace and to give vitamin B and cardiac medication or to inject calcium. This approach treats a large segment of this disease complex. In addition, it is advisable that those animals that frequently suffer from this disorder be excluded from further breeding.

Cardiac damage and circulatory disorders are problems that are not uncommon in chinchillas. Again, we have to decide first of all whether we are witnessing the actual cause or whether these are peripheral symptoms. Infections, injuries, difficult births, and physically demanding diseases place much stress on the circulatory system. This stress can lead to permanent heart damage or even cardiac arrest. In this case it would be wrong to treat primarily for circulatory disorder and to ignore the primary disease problem. The circulatory system in chinchillas as in many undomesticated animals, is rather fragile. Often it takes only minor stress that would have no effect at all on domesticated animals to induce a circulatory collapse.

Many animals with a history of convulsions have shown during an autopsy a conspicuous and substantial enlargement of the suprarenal. It is indeed possible that such disorders are hormone-related. A treatment in this direction should be tried out (ACTH, cortisone).

Occasionally breeders report "feeding convulsions" in which animals that are fed last because they occupy the last cages in a breeding enclosure sometimes display spasms. It is recommended that these then be fed first or they should be fed separately.

It has also happened that an animal that is being evaluated went into shock when exposed to the bright light used by the evaluator (so-called "light shock"). A similar shock can be incurred during tattooing. If these animals are returned to their cage and left alone they will quickly recover. Animals like this, however, should be kept under observation by the breeder in order to determine whether they also go into convulsions under other circumstances.

# 7) Infectious Diseases and Parasites

## INFECTIOUS DISEASES

The greatest concern among all those who keep animals is always infectious diseases, especially when these occur in the form of epidemics. Nobody knows where they come from or when they are coming; suddenly one or more animals get sick, they become weak and listless, or one morning they are simply found dead in the cage. Before the correct counter-measures can be initiated more animals get sick or even die.

In chinc! illas and small mammals, providing the necessary help in time is particularly difficult since comprehensive examinations cannot be made. Therefore, it is often recognized too late that the animals are seriously ill. *Prevention* still remains the most effective measure against infectious diseases:

—thorough cleanliness of animals and their accommodations;

—providing favorable climatic conditions;

—an optimum diet;

—protective immunization whenever possible.


Newly purchased animals must initially be isolated for a few weeks from the rest of the stock in order to keep out undetected disease pathogens.

At this point it must be stressed that not all diseases referred to as being infectious are necessarily that. Even when antibiotics and sulfonamides have actually induced healing, this does not mean that the particular disease was indeed in-

96

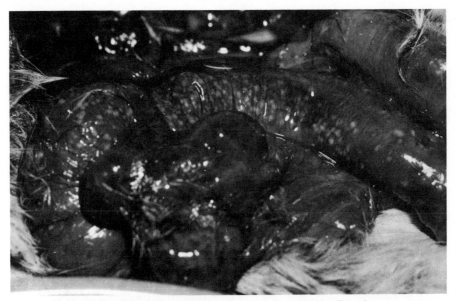

Colon of *Chinchilla lanigera* female with necrosis caused by *Pseudomonas aeruginosa*. These organs enabled the Animal Hygiene Institute of the University of Munich to establish pure listeriosis cultures.

fectious. If animals in a certain group become sick and there is indeed a suspicion of an infection, *all* animals must be closely examined. If the majority of animals fall ill or are suspected of becoming ill it does not make any sense to separate the "healthy ones" from the "sick ones." This is only required when individual animals in a large facility are sick.

When an animal picks up an infectious pathogen it will not — in most cases — become visibly ill until some time later. This interval between infection and the actual outbreak of the disease is called the *incubation period*. Consequently, if the largest proportion of stock of a breeding facility has fallen ill, transferring those animals not yet visibly ill would only mean transmitting the disease to other rooms or enclosures that may soon be needed as quarantine facilities for new animals that may have to be purchased. Instead, dead animals and their cages and associated equipment must always be promptly removed. The "contaminated" facilities must remain empty until they have been thoroughly cleaned and repeatedly disinfected.

An important step in eradicating a disease is a preliminary autopsy of those animals that have already died. This has proved to be the best method of obtaining correct diagnosis and thus be able to initiate the necessary treatment. There should be no doubt that all this must be left to the professional experience and competence of a veterinarian. Even a veterinarian without any chinchilla experience can under these circumstances still be more effective than a layman.

We are now coming to a discussion of some of the most important infectious diseases of chinchillas. All infectious diseases known so far are caused by bacteria or their close relatives. There are only individual, scattered reports of possible virus infections as the causes of infectious diseases.

## LISTERIOSIS

Listeriosis is an infectious disease found worldwide in man and animals. The pathogens are extraordinarily resistant bacteria that can survive for long periods in water, soil, or feces, even under extreme temperature conditions. Mainly ruminants and rodents become infected; the latter include chinchillas. Although there have been some stock infections, it is *not a typical chinchilla disease,* since the majority of established breeding facilities are free of listeriosis. But if there is a disregard for the basic rules of hygiene and the pathogen is introduced it can spread relatively easily throughout the entire stock.

In chinchillas the disease nearly always spreads from the digestive tract. The animals become infected via the mouth by feeding on feces or contaminated food, and the usually very sensitive intestinal mucous membrane offers the pathogen easy access to the body. Usually several animals get sick simultaneously or in quick succession and the disease lasts a long time. The *incubation period* is relatively short, five to eight days. Unfortunately, the usual disease manifestations are rather inconspicuous. The overall well-being of the animal is disturbed, it is apathetic, and it feeds poorly or not at all. In acute cases death can occur within a few days. Soft feces over a prolonged period of time and possible intestinal prolapse are symptoms of a chronic case of listeriosis. In its "nervous" form, listeriosis is particularly conspicuous; then

98

it is accompanied by loss of equilibrium, staggering around, an unsteady walk, and similar symptoms. Trying to find out how listeriosis was introduced into a facility is virtually impossible.

When a bacteriological examination has revealed the presence of listeriosis in a facility, all animals must be included in the treatment plan. This is absolutely essential, since some time elapses between the pathogen entering the body and when it becomes possible to detect the disease. Regrettably, it must also be admitted that treatment for listeriosis is not always successful. This is primarily due to the fact that in chinchillas it can never be detected sufficiently early, and treatment usually does not commence until there are severe general symptoms. Most effective are sulfonamides and broad-spectrum antibiotics (tetracycline and chlortetracycline).

Hygiene is of paramount importance in these cases. The healthy animals are always serviced first and then the sick ones. Strict separation of food, dust baths, and equipment between cages is advisable. Cages should only be restocked after they have been thoroughly cleaned *and* disinfected. Since the listeriosis pathogen are very resistant, the most effective method is the application of heat above 60°C (140°F). Merely leaving cages empty even over prolonged periods of time does not have a reliable bactericidal effect.

If the listeriosis infection is acute, purulent areas on the tongues of the animals can be evidence of the disease. In this case the animals must also be examined for dental anomalies since these can cause mechanical damage to the tongue and oral mucous membrane. Should this have happened it is also possible that listeriosis could have occurred as a secondary infection.

## PASTEURELLA

Bacteria of the genus *Pasteurella* can cause infectious diseases in many animal species as well as in humans. In chinchillas and other herbivorous rodents it causes the disease known as pasteurellosis, pseudotuberculosis, or yersiniosis . Transmission takes place through direct contact between animals or through pathogen transmission via the food. The incubation period in chinchillas is eight to 14 days.

The clinical symptoms in living infected animals include apathy, loss of condition, and gastrointestinal disorders with diarrhea and constipation. There may also be some cases of intestinal prolapse. Since this disease is accompanied by fever, pulse rate and respiratory rate are distinctly increased. The symptoms are non-specific, so a definitive diagnosis is rarely possible on a live animal. Therefore, when deaths occur it is essential that a detailed autopsy, including a bacteriological investigation, be made.

### PSEUDOMONAS AERUGINOSA

Bacteria of the genus *Pseudomonas* are widely distributed in nature. They have been identified bacteriologically as the pathogens in many diseases affecting man and animals. *Pseudomonas aeruginosa* infections in chinchillas are very similar in their external manifestations to listeriosis, rodentiosis, or

Two *C. lanigera* stomachs cut open. Left: Stomach from a healthy animal as a comparison with the right stomach, which contains numerous small and large hemorrhaging patches in the mucous membrane due to infection by *Pseudomonas aeruginosa*.

100

gastrointestinal disorders because of abnormal bacterial flora. On one hand, there can be an acute form manifesting itself in the form of "blood poisoning"; on the other hand, a chronic form affects individual organs. For instance, it can happen that several animals in a single facility suddenly die, while others show progressive loss of condition, variable feces consistency, intestinal prolapse, or spontaneous abortions. Obviously the entire scale of possible disease symptoms can appear in chinchillas without having symptoms typical for a specific infection. Spontaneous abortions can also be due to other external influences and can occur without an infection being present.

Epidemic infectious diseases with externally similar symptoms cannot always be individually distinguished, and bacteriological tests are required for a definitive diagnosis. Therefore, the treatment of infected chinchillas is difficult because without explicit bacteriological test results a specific therapy can not be initiated. Even prophylactic measures against this complex of infectious diseases have to be adapted accordingly.

## OTHER INFECTIONS

Apart from the already mentioned epidemic infectious diseases, the following diseases have also been reported in chinchillas: nocardiosis (streptotrichosis, a septicemic streptococcus infection), histoplasmosis, leptospirosis, and toxoplosmosis. The infectious pathways of these diseases are not clearly understood. Presumably contaminated food or contact with already infected animals may be the cause. In many cases young animals or those with a lowered resistance following transport or a change of diet are particularly susceptible.

Of these, *histoplasmosis* is clinically the most likely recognizable condition since affected chinchillas invariably display symptoms of anemia. The presence of *toxoplasmosis* can possibly be indicated by disorders of the central nervous system such as loss of equilibrium, abnormal positioning of the head, or other attacks that suggest this disease. Here it must be remembered that similar manifestations can also occur with cardiac and circulatory diseases. Jaundice can be indica-

101

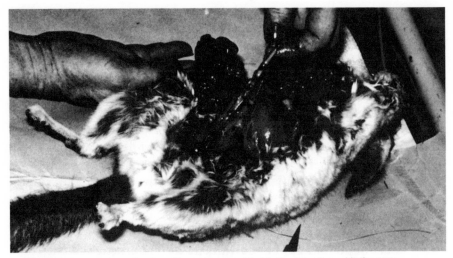

A case of severe constipation. The upper hand holds the intestine with the remnant of normal feces. The lower hand raises the cecum (blind gut), which clearly shows that it is blocked by serious constipation.

tive of *leptospirosis,* but this symptom also often accompanies diet-related liver disorders. Chinchillas are supposed to be particularly susceptible to *Leptospira pomona,* the causative organism.

There are also reports on the occurrence of *leucosis* (leukemia) in chinchillas. Since this has been found to be transmitted by viruses in other animals, chinchillas infected by this disease should be put down and their progeny closely monitored. The diagnosis is by means of blood tests, and there is no known treatment!

## RESPIRATORY TRACT INFECTIONS

Some ear and lung diseases in chinchillas seem to be virus-related, but their diagnosis is difficult and even then the result is unclear (in the absence of bacteria). If bacteria are found they may be part of a secondary infection after the mucous membranes have lost their resistance because of the virus infection. In many cases fungi can also be the causative agents of respiratory diseases, but commonly bacteria of the genera *Streptococcus* and *Pneumococcus* are involved.

Regardless of the pathogen involved, the clinical picture is invariably similar. Usually there is a watery or purulent nasal discharge together with labored breathing. In cases of serious lung infections there is also substantial stress on the heart and circulatory system, and it is their eventual failure that is usually the cause of death.

These diseases usually do not occur as epidemics; they affect primarily young animals. If there is any eye or nasal discharge one should also consider dental anomalies. If the chinchilla breeder is able to get a rectal temperature reading from an affected animal, an elevated temperature of 40° to 41°C (104°F) is indicative of such an infectious disease.

## GASTROINTESTINAL DISORDERS

Gastrointestinal problems manifest themselves either as constipation or diarrhea. Clinically there are symptoms of a cholic. It must be noted here that the cases of *constipation* are often recognized too late. When two or more animals are kept together in the same cage it is hardly possible to monitor the feces accurately. Constipation is best diagnosed by palpating the abdomen of any affected animal, but matters can become complicated by, for instance, a pregnant female.

On the other hand, *diarrhea* is easily and quickly recognized. Feces consistency and a mucus-coated anal region are unmistakable signs. The primary causes for this condition are usually an inappropriate diet and faulty husbandry practices. Of course, constipation as well as diarrhea can also be a symptom of an infectious disease. The intestinal wall and mucous membrane lose their functional ability partially or completely, which then leads to these sorts of disorders. In order to determine the cause one should first scrutinize the diet and the overall maintenance conditions. All food items that have recently come into use or those that are hard to digest must be omitted for the time being. Moreover, it is advisable that this measure be applied to the *entire* stock, because prevention is better than any cure! Beyond that, other measures that may need to be taken depend upon the practices in a particular breeding facility.

In any event, it is always advisable to initiate a bacteriological fecal examination, animals that have died should be autopsied, and consideration should be given to possible causes of the disease such as food poisoning or incorrect medication.

*Constipation* must be treated quickly and intensively, otherwise this condition becomes difficult to control. Soothing, cramp-relieving, and peristalsis-promoting medications have proven to be effective. Lentin (carbachol) must not be given to chinchillas because it is too harsh and can easily tear the intestine; moreover, it not only acts upon the smooth muscles of the intestine but also affects the uterus, and pregnant females will often spontaneously abort after having been given this medication. It is very important, however, that constipation be alleviated. This is most effectively (and harmlessly) accomplished by giving paraffin (kerosine) orally and at the same time as an enema. The oil softens the hardened feces, and when this is further supported by heat and gentle massaging it soon corrects this unpleasant intestinal disorder. Be careful, though, when massaging the abdomen of pregnant females that are quite obviously pregnant! Beyond that, an attempt must be made to find the actual cause of constipation or diarrhea, which must then be treated. It is important that the balance of the intestinal flora is either maintained or re-established as quickly as possible.

The liver, spleen, and kidneys — digestive, filtering, and excretory organs — are all more or less related to the digestive tract and its functions. The infections and other diseases mentioned in this chapter often place much stress upon the liver in chinchillas. It is essentially impossible to provide effective medical help because of the absence of a definitive diagnosis. However, in those cases where one suspects problems it is often advantageous to initiate a prophylactic liver therapy.

It must be emphasized that the majority of gastrointestinal diseases are not primarily infectious but instead are caused by faulty husbandry procedures, even though an imbalance in the intestinal flora found during an autopsy may indicate to the layman that this is not so. Every detrimental influence upon the gastrointestinal tract effects a change in the intestinal flora.

The key problem lies in the fact that healthy chinchillas do not have *Escherichia (E. coli)* bacteria within their intestinal

104

Feces from a healthy *C. lanigera.*

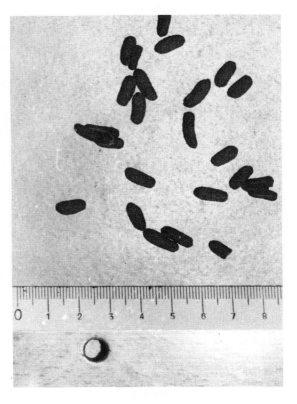

**Below:** Samples 1 and 2 display types of normal feces; a healthy digestive tract. Sample 3: The feces are longish, thin, and bent, a sign of constipation. Sample 4: Feces are short, pointed, and hard; very serious case of constipation due to an intestinal inflammation.

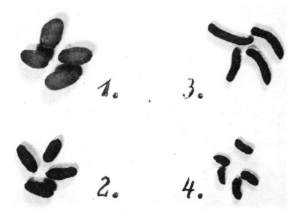

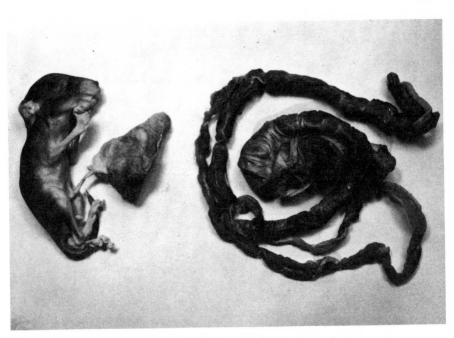

*Left:* A nearly full-term embryo from a female that died of a case of extreme constipation. *Right:* The intestine was extensively dehydrated in order to show the hard, dark feces blockages.

flora, but this bacterium is present virtually everywhere else. It can easily be picked up by chinchillas via drinking water and feed or dirty equipment and cages when there is even the slightest violation of sound hygienic practices. When there is a weakness in the gastrointestinal tract and/or the intestinal mucous membrane, these bacteria can then readily cause diseases. Therefore, the most common causes of death or disease in chinchillas are gastrointestinal disorders that are the result of feeding and maintenance mistakes.

Under constant climatic and dietary conditions chinchillas are relatively easy to keep. If there is a partial change in one of these factors, individual highly susceptible or weakened animals will soon become sick. If there are major changes, there can then be sudden losses, where an autopsy will invariably show an infection of the gastrointestinal tract. The animals are alert and active, and then suddenly one animal refuses food and it may well be dead within the hour. The bacteriological test result is invariably *Pseudomonas aerugi-*

*nosa, Proteus vulgaris, Escherichia coli,* or similar pathogens.

Rectal prolapse is common unless the animals die quickly. Intestinal invaginations, which are not visible externally, can also occur anywhere along the intestine. Generally there is little a veterinarian can do, since chinchillas in this condition usually get to a veterinarian far too late. This is not necessarily the fault of the breeder, but instead it is due to the complex circumstances that make early recognition and awareness of the severity of the disease largely impossible — it is usually already too late when the first symptoms appear. Besides, these diseases are also rarely curable even in other animal species. Some breeders insist that they have had success with treatments using their own methods, but I believe that it is advisable with these problems to seek professional veterinary help as quickly as possible. Treatment should always be attempted.

Digestive tract of a chinchilla (fixed in formalin) with intestinal inversion and prolapse (center of illustration).

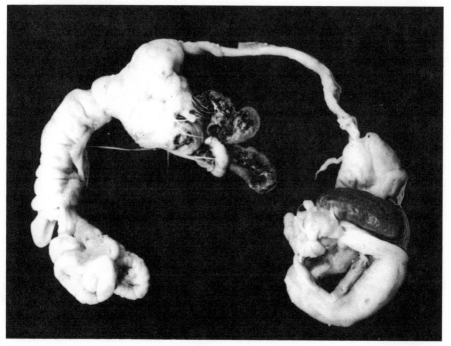

107

## COMMENTS ABOUT MEDICATION

Certain peculiarities of some animal species may make it necessary to implement treatment methods other than those that are commonly used. Experience with chinchillas has shown that administering medication orally, particularly for the very common gastrointestinal disorders, is more effective than injections. Also, the great sensitivity of these animals makes them seem more conducive to stress from injections in general than from the giving of drops and tablets. Drops and tablets can easily be administered in conjunction with food so that the medication is not even detected, while an injection always requires intensive manipulation of the patient.

I have seen a chinchilla being offered a medicine tablet to "sniff on" to see whether the smell is acceptable, then suddenly take the tablet in its front paws and start gnawing on it. I have animals that will eagerly lick up drops offered on dried bread, although the drops have an obnoxious odor and

Giving medication orally.

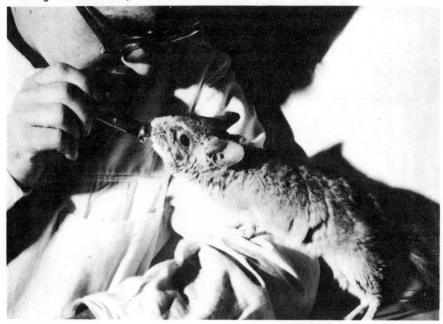

How to hold a fully grown chinchilla while administering medication via pipette.

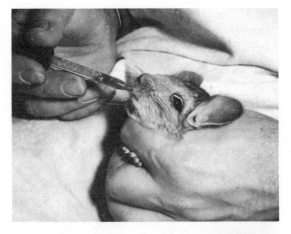

Auto mutilation after an intramuscular injection of too much (1 ml) of an incompatible medication.

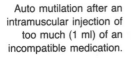

Abscesses and necrosis of the skin following subcutaneous injection of an incompatible medication.

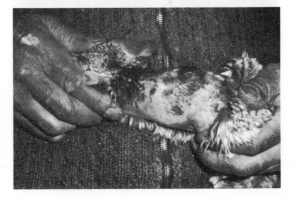

taste to humans. These are some simple methods of giving medication to chinchillas. Drops and ground-up tablets can also be mixed into the food and in drinking water or put on raisins. This way the medication is usually taken without objection.

There are, however, chinchillas that are either too stubborn or already too weak to take medication by the simple methods. Then we have to use pipettes or syringes. Since rodents have very sharp cutting teeth, it is advisable to use pipettes or syringes made of plastic. Glass pipettes are often fractured no matter how carefully they are being handled. The filled pipette or syringe is inserted into a corner of the mouth, behind the gnawing teeth. (If it is inserted between the molars it will be chewed to pieces.) Then with slight but steady pressure the solution or suspension is delivered into the oral cavity drop by drop. Special care must be taken that the animal actually swallows the liquid, otherwise it may end up in the lungs, leading to an incurable foreign body pneumonia.

It is generally truthful to say that all those medications that are normally used on other mammals can also be used on chinchillas. Breeders should not engage in experimentation! Anyone using a particular medication must be aware beforehand of the correct dosages to be used. If there are no previous experiences with a particular medication and its compatibility in chinchillas, it is advisable to use dosages relative to those recommended for other species.

It would be stating the obvious to say that too much medication is harmful while not enough is ineffective. If injections must be given to chinchillas, this should be done under the skin (subcutaneously), which can damage the pelt; into the musculature of the upper thigh (intramuscular), up to 0.5 ml per thigh; or into the abdominal cavity (intraperitoneal). As already mentioned above, however, in chinchillas I prefer to give medication orally. Administering injections should always be left to a veterinarian because a number of important points must be taken into consideration.

## ADMINISTERING MEDICATION

First a few general comments about administering medica-

110

tion to chinchillas. Since pelt quality is the prime objective for most breeders of these animals, we must not do anything that could damage the skin and so also damage the fur. This means that injections have to be given at a site where adverse effects of the medication do not show and will not have any later detrimental effect on pelt quality. The only suitable places for subcutaneous injections are the side of the neck and the inside of the thighs. Intramuscular injections in chinchillas are always given into the thigh. Only under extreme circumstances should the volume injected exceed 0.5 ml. One has to remember that such a large volume can cause localized damage to the pelt. Independent of the volume injected, pelt damage can also occur when substances are used that are not compatible or only marginally compatible, such as substances that in humans or other animal species briefly cause pain due to the solvents used. Medications that include local anesthetics must never be administered to chinchillas. These anesthetics are invariably effective only in dosages too high for chinchillas and thus induce intoxication, which can be fatal.

Although *peroral (p.o.) administration* of medication (tablets or liquids) causes the least amount of tissue damage, it is not always as effective as an injection, presuming, of course, that the chinchilla actually takes the medication. Chinchillas that are simply too weak and have ceased feeding cannot be given medication in food or water. Moreover, one has to remember that in an enclosure with several animals an accurate oral dosage of medication is not assured unless the medication is given individually to each animal.

## STRESS

The first step in the treatment of all diseases is to eliminate the cause. Often this requires the sixth sense of a detective as well as scrutinizing deliberation in order to find the real problem. To change the diet when diseases are present is wrong. The most you should do is reduce the amount of food offered. For instance, it is advisable to give only hay, low-protein and low-fat food (pellets do not meet these requirements), and drinking water to sick chinchillas. Regular food intake is particularly important. Even the best medicine does not protect against starvation. Loss of condition can be due to not only a disease but also may be a response to poor food intake. Even the best-treated chinchilla will be dead within two days without food.

During the months of February, March, August, September, and October, chinchillas must not be placed under any stress. A change of diet (deliberately or unintentionally), formation of new breeding pairs, or moving the cage could endanger the already fragile constitution of chinchillas. This means, for instance, that during these critical periods the breeder must not start to feed fresh hay but instead must have an ample supply of last year's crop. More specifically, a change over from one brand of pellets to another must be avoided. Any peculiar reaction or behavior of the animals during these periods must be taken seriously, and it is better to treat an animal too early rather than too late.

## TREATMENTS

Medical treatments for those diseases discussed have — with a few exceptions — already been published elsewhere. The data available clearly show that the most common causes for diseases and mortalities (especially during the critical time periods) are diseases of the gastrointestinal tract. Bacteriological tests in all of these cases indicated that pathogenic strains of *Escherichia coli* and *Pseudomonas aeruginosa* caused the fatal diseases. Resistance indicators (the testing of different medications for their effectiveness against the bacteria) have shown that antibiotics and sulfonamides are the most effective and at the same time they are also totally harmless to chinchillas. Practical application has confirmed this.

We can treat sick chinchillas with *chloramphenicol* (Chloromycetin or Leucomycin). 300 mg per animal per day is the recommended dosage for gastrointestinal problems. *Neomycin, Spectinomycin* and some similar drugs are also effective.

In some instances there is still insufficient data on hand. *Ampicillin* injections, for instance, are alleged to have side effects such as apathy and a loss of appetite. On the other hand, this antibiotic is often indispensable because of increasing pathogen resistance. Often Ampicillin is the only effective medication available. When tetracycline is used one has to remember that this substance can also damage intestinal flora and discolor the teeth of young chinchillas yellow.

*Sulfonamides* can be used in chinchillas, preferably dissolved in drinking water. Since most infections in chinchillas are caused by *Escherichia coli, Pseudomonas aeruginosa* and similar bacteria, Colistin has proven to be particularly effective. A combination of this with sulfonamides can also be administered. This is the medium of choice in the majority of chinchilla diseases. Apart from a specific therapy for infectious diseases, symptomatic treatment must also be initiated.

It is recommended that during the critical periods endangered stocks are given Colistin as a prophylactic. For instance, before and after transport or for changes in maintenance procedures and/or diet modifications the animals should be given Colistin for two or three days.

## IMMUNIZATION

Immunization is an effective method for the prevention of epidemic infectious bacterial diseases, if administered correctly. The breeder has to make sure that the animals that are to be immunized are perfectly healthy. This is not always easy. Unfortunately, we can never really tell on living animals whether they are completely healthy or whether there is already a subclinical infection, the onset of a disease. Consequently, if a breeder does not know his animals very well and through observations is not able to ascertain whether they are healthy or not, then the immunization carries a certain risk. Nevertheless, one should take advantage of its benefits, especially in those facilities where mortalities due to bacterial diseases are not uncommon.

Beyond that, it must be remembered that very young chinchillas should not be immunized. The stress involved can be too severe. Also, young chinchillas are not able to dvelop an effective immunity until some time later in their development. The best procedure is to immunize presumably healthy chinchillas only when they are at least 12 weeks old. The vaccine manufacturer's recommendations must be followed closely. In all cases where there is any doubt about the health status of the animals, they should be placed into quarantine for at least 10 to 14 days before they are immunized.

Immunization, of course, does not protect against the consequences of poor husbandry practices or an inadequate diet. Moreover, it is not a license for carelessness or disregard of proper hygienic standards in a chinchilla breeding facility.

Constantly recurring bacterial infections in chinchillas have given rise to the thought that prophylactic vaccinations can inhibit the outbreak of epidemics. For that purpose a laboratory in the United States has developed a vaccine (Chin-Vac) that acts on some of the most common bacterial pathogens in chinchillas, which are primarily *Streptococcus pyogenes*, *Salmonella typhimurium*, *Pseudomonas aeruginosa*, and *Pasteurella multicida*. This vaccine is also available in Europe. It is administered intramuscularly to chinchillas that are older than 30 days. The dosage depends on the actual age of the animal. The basic immunization consists of a series of three injections given within 21 to 28 days, followed by an annual booster shot. So far it has been shown that this immunization provides effective protection against epidemic bacterial infections. Again, it must be emphasized that only healthy animals should be given this vaccine.

Beyond that, there seems to be evidence that certain pathogens in different geographical regions can develop specific local strains. For that reason a vaccine was developed in West Germany from pathogens taken from chinchillas that died there. These are *Proteus vulgaris*, *Pseudomonas aeruginosa*, *Pasteurella pseudotuberculosis*, *Listeria monocytogens*, and *Escherichia coli*. In principle it is the same vaccine as that manufactured in the United States, but made from somewhat different pathogens or strains of pathogens. For this vaccine the manufacturer recommends two initial injections at intervals of two to three weeks. The animals must be at least six to eight weeks old, though preferably in excess of 12 weeks. The dosage is 0.5 ml, administered subcutaneously.

A further method of immunization against bacterial diseases is the oral administration of a Coli-Mix-Vaccine. This is given via drinking water over a period of ten days. Allegedly, immunity is obtained within four days after the start of immunization. Here, too, sound hygienic measures have to be observed.

114

Another method of prevention is the use of a so-called autovaccine. The pathogens used in this vaccine are isolated from the organs of the diseased and dead animals and then injected into the entire stock. Another method of prophylaxis is the establishment of "para-immunity."

Wherever diseases do not respond to the methods of classical medicine and a generally weakened body resistance is suspected, it is sensible to support and stimulate the body's own defense mechanism. This is an ancient method that has been somewhat forgotten about. Since the overall immunity can be improved within hours with this method, it is also suitable as support in the treatment of infectious diseases. It utilizes proteins (blood, milk, and others) or medications used in "non-specific stimulation therapy." Vitamins are also very effective. Special para-immunity inducers are currently being developed and should be used following a case-by-case evaluation.

Ventral view of upper jaws of *Chinchilla*; skull in the center with normal tooth position.

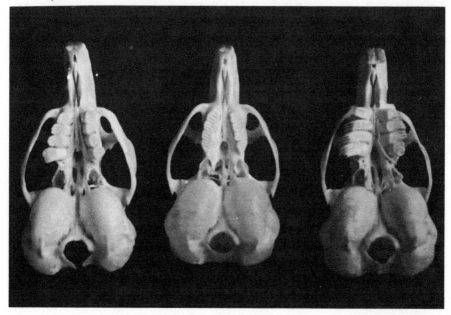

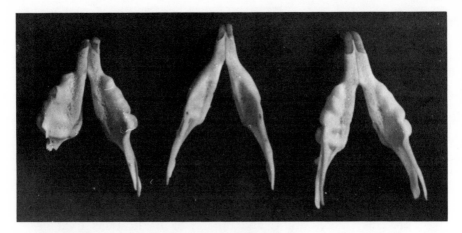

**Above:** Lower jaws of *Chinchilla*. Note abnormal bone growth in the area of the tooth sockets in the two outer lower jaws. **Below:** High-grade tooth anomaly.

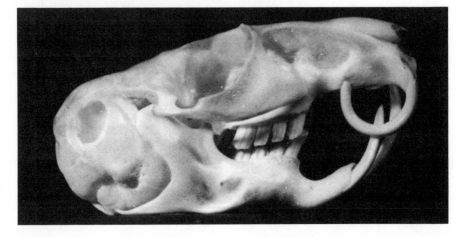

## DENTAL ANOMALIES

I commonly encounter animals with watering eyes and unable to feed properly. Invariably the breeder concerned has tried repeatedly to file or clip the gnawing teeth (incisors) since they had become too long. Unfortunately, that approach does not work, not even temporarily. Other breeders may try to provide relief by administering antibiotics (Aureomycon, Terramycin) on advice from veterinarian, druggists, or laymen.

116

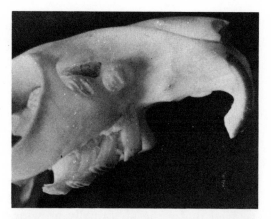

Lateral view of skull. The molars have grown outward, the tooth roots have penetrated the bone, and the incisors are inadequately worn down.

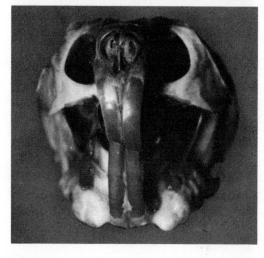

An extreme dental condition. Looked at from the front all that is noticeable is the unusual sloping wear on the incisors.

Usually it turns out that these animals suffer from substantial anomalies of the molars (cheek teeth). Changes in the gnawing teeth (incisors) are of a secondary nature since usually their abnormalities result from their not being worn down properly. Consequently, in cases like this it is totally wrong to shorten the incisors, since this ignores the real problem. Even if molars that have grown up and out or down and are straightened, not much is gained. In these cases the roots have grown out of their alveoli and through the bone into the chewing musculature. The dental problems may — in part — be the cause of watering eyes; in fact, this condition may even turn into a purulent oral inflammation.

Other authors believe a *Pseudomonas* infection to be the

117

cause, although we presumably are dealing with a secondary infection. The outwardly growing teeth eventually damage the oral mucous membrane, thus causing purulent abscesses in the oral cavity. In my experience there is little that can be done once this stage has been reached. The animal can no longer feed because the molars no longer have a proper grinding surface. The incorrectly growing teeth have damaged the mucous membrane, and the incorrectly growing roots press against the chewing musculature, its blood vessels, and its nerves. This sort of abnormal dental development can go to such extremes that the tongue becomes wedged under the abnormally growing molars of the lower jaw and the animal is unable to swallow.

Such problems are often further compounded by the fact that the bones in the upper and lower jaw are porous, which can lead to enormous swellings along the jaw. Understandably, all these processes are very painful to the animal. Here it should also be noted that these tooth anomalies are hereditary; there are records of as many as three successive generation with dental problems of this nature. An unfavorable diet

Schematic otoscope pictures made while checking the molars of *Chinchilla lanigera*. a) Normal tooth position viewed from the front. b) Onset of dental anomaly. c) Extreme dental anomaly.

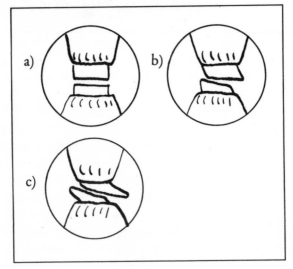

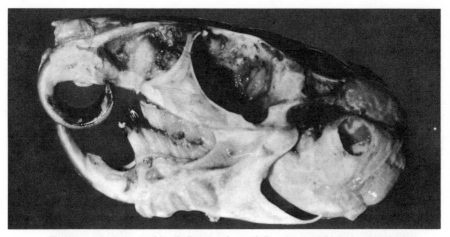

The upper incisors in this skull are only partially worn and in their posterior upward growth they are already touching the roof of the palate. This animal died of listeriosis, which in my opinion must in this case be considered as a secondary infection.

(pellets included) can further enhance such abnormal growth patterns.

In essence then, we are dealing here with excessive growth processes of the incisors and molars in the upper as well as lower jaws, which can be hereditary. In advanced stages these problems can no longer be treated and corrected. Early mechanical elimination of excessive growth on the incisors and the sharp edges on the molars can only be done with great difficulty and under general anesthesia. Unfortunately, this risky and uneconomical procedure will not remedy the underlying cause, and an incorrect diet will promote an even more rapid return of this problem. Beyond that, there is usually already a secondary infection. Merely shortening the incisors does not have any favorable effect on this disease.

The most important thing is to recognize dental anomalies early. An otoscope as used for ear examinations in man and animals is ideal for this purpose. The illuminated funnel can easily be inserted between the incisors and the mucous membrane of the cheek wall to look at the anterior molars. In healthy animals these teeth protrude 1-2 mm above the gum and have a smooth, level chewing (macerating) surface. In chinchillas that suffer from the above-mentioned tooth problems the teeth in the upper jaw have a club-shaped appendage or a sharp edge and turn toward the outside. There is then either a sloping chewing surface or none at all. When the incisors are not artificially regulated, their excessive length and their often yellow coloration (instead of white) are indicative of changes in the molars. An examination with an otoscope will give a definitive answer.

Unfortunately, it has been my experience that there is usually very little that can be done for chinchillas that suffer from this disorder. Therefore, it is important that an early diagnosis is made so that the animal does not suffer needlessly. Consequently, each newly acquired animal should be checked first for dental problems and thereafter it should be closely monitored. It could be that certain dental problems may have been previously corrected, at least on the molars, so small anomalies are not recognizable at the time of examination. When chewing difficulties develop soon after purchase it is concrete evidence of tooth anomalies that were overlooked. Proof of the hereditary nature of dental anomalies still requires additional material. Nevertheless, animals with these problems must not be used for breeding.

Regrettably, these days breeders do not pay enough attention to dental problems, so many chinchillas die a painful death. Essentially these animals starve to death since they are no longer able to feed, and the developing wounds become subject to secondary infections. Chinchillas that have watering eyes, feed poorly, or make excessive chewing movements during food intake, or which discharge saliva possibly containing blood must always be suspected of tooth anomalies and must be carefully examined!

Apart from these anatomical anomalies, foreign particles (pieces of bar, grain hulls, chaff, and other little things) can become wedged between the teeth or stuck in the larynx and esophagus (pieces of wood, seed grains), which may make feeding difficult or completely impossible. An otoscope examination of the oral cavity usually reveals the cause. The foreign body normally can be removed with a pair of forceps.

Pieces of wood or seeds in the larynx or pharynx are usually found only during an autopsy. In live animals the displays of choking or great restlessness are signs of such a foreign body being present. Unfortunately, in most of these cases there is little the breeder can do.

## PARASITES

The literature (especially American publications) contains a number of publications on parasites in chinchillas, but parasites actually are not common. There are only a few reports from Europe on parasitic infestations in chinchillas. In fact, there has only been one case of stomach worms (*Haemonchus contortus*). Infestation occurred via green food that was contaminated with strongylid-containing sheep feces. Beyond that, there have been two cases of cysticercosis of the liver in chinchillas; both animals had been imported from America with neoplasms the size of chicken eggs on the liver. A few tapeworms and nematodes are recorded from chinchillas but they usually present no problems.

There are still divided opinions on the occurrence of *Giardia duodenale* and its function in the duodenum of chinchillas. The presence of these single-celled organisms was con-

*C. lanigera* liver with new growth due to tapeworm infestation (cysticercosis) of the liver.

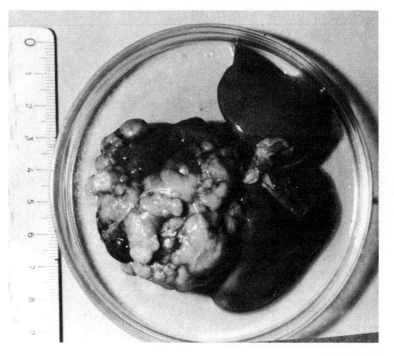

firmed through tests made at the University of Munich. Some workers believe that the presence of *Giardia* in the duodenum of chinchillas should be considered as being pathological, requiring appropriate treatment. Certainly a massive infestation of *Giardia*, especially in young animals with diarrhea, is pathological and treatment is recommended with Acranil, 20-25 mg/day/animal for one week, or with Atebrin.

A growing pelt of *Chinchilla lanigera* with insufficient density; the band of new hair growth is clearly visible.

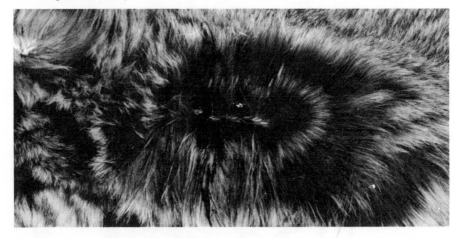

# 8) Skin and Fur Problems

Since most breeders keep chinchillas as fur-bearing animals, it is understandable that they are particularly interested in the condition of the pelt. Once again, it must be said that as far as skin and pelt are concerned, chinchillas are not subject to particular species-specific diseases but instead only to variations of some already well-known diseases. In reference to damage and diseases to skin and fur some clearly delineated terms must be defined. Specific skin diseases may occur in chinchillas just as well as in other animal species, but so far there is little evidence of these.

## INFLAMMATIONS
Inflammations and eczema from injuries and scratch wounds must be treated the same way as in other animals. Of course, the fur is always more or less affected. Sometimes supposed fur damage is just a side effect of an unrelated disease, so you must not forget to look for the cause of such damage before initiating treatment. If an animal has an inadequate coat the skin must be examined first and foremost. If we find changes in the skin that require treatment the fur has to be shorn away or hair tufts pulled out over the affected area up to the surrounding healthy areas. Treatment through the fur is useless and can even lead to secondary damage. Inflammations of the skin are treated with anti-flammatory or infection-inhibiting ointments or suspensions. For eczemas one prefers to use mild ointments or liniments.

## FUR BREAKING
Fur breaking can be described as a type of fur or pelt damage in which the animals have "holes" in their pelt that can

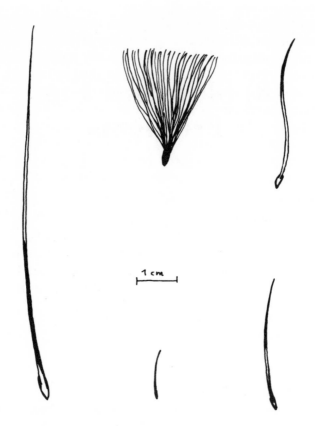

Various types of hair in *Chinchilla lanigera* depicted in proper size relationships.

cover wide areas of the body. The posterior regions are most commonly affected. The animals are then no longer silvery gray, but blue instead. A cause for this disorder has not yet been found, in spite of intensive research. Parasites, fungi, and changes in the skin have not been implicated. A characteristic of this "disease" is the fact that if an affected animal is kept under optimum conditions and is given a nutritionally adequate diet the fur will regrow flawlessly within six to 12 months.

Since nutrition seems to play a large role in this, laymen have concluded that this skin disorder must be a deficiency syndrome. It is not easy to contradict such an opinion. Presumably what is happening is that the affected animals are suffering from extended or physiologically impaired molting. All animals with some sort of hair coat shed and regrow (i.e., molt) their hair in a well-defined, natural cycle. Artificially produced environmental conditions can lead to significant disturbances. This can manifest itself in large-scale loss of hair or excessive growth of one type of hair with a simultaneous retardation of another type of hair. It cannot be denied that the composition of the diet and the maintenance condition play a very significant role in all this. The recommended treatment is a nutritionally balanced diet with minerals, stored in a cool, dry area. Usually normal hair growth will eventually restore the original condition of the pelt.

## FUR BITING

Particularly unpleasant in any chinchilla breeding facilities are the "fur biters." These can be animals of either sex that bite off the hairs of their pelt. Usually they chew on their

*Chinchilla lanigera* female with diffuse hair loss (excessive molting).

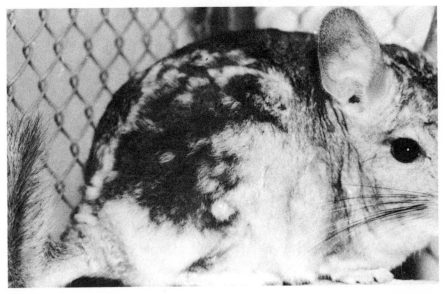

own fur, but chewing on other animals is found, though fairly rare. Similar problems are known in chickens and cage birds, where it is generally known as feather biting. Such fur bites can upset the entire breeding group.

It must be emphasized here that only those animals that are actually caught tearing out tufts of hair or gnawing on hair can legitimately be described as fur biters. They must also exhibit the typical fur biter appearance: as far as the mouth can reach all the wool hairs have been gnawed off, and only the short dark hair stumps of the lower fur zones are visible. Only the hairs on the head, neck, and tail remain intact, and the animal has a "lion's mane." If other animals in the same group are also being bitten, the fur biter will chew on all sorts of places along the body of its mates, which can then be mistaken for "fur breakers."

If one follows the growth of young from fur biter parents, one often finds (even in artificially reared young and those kept separate from parents and siblings) a period of fur biting at an age of about two months. The young will chew on their own pelt or try to do it to others if kept in groups. However, this behavior disappears again after eight to 14 days (as observed in five young with such a heriditary predisposition). Within another eight to nine months fur biting in these animals could usually no longer be observed.

When fur biters are closely examined there is nothing unusual about their skin and hair. Cultures for fungus invariably turn out negative. It appears strange, however, that in chinchillas, and particularly in fur biters, one does not find trichobezoares (so-called hair stones) in the intestines. These hair stones (common in other herbivorous animals) develop from hair balls (formed through licking the fur) in the stomach that accumulate salt deposits. Eventually a round stone develops which may lead to an intestinal blockage. Anyway, no one has yet succeeded in identifying a fur biter on the basis of it stomach content (large amount of hair).

On the other hand, fur biters often display changes in their suprarenals, together with an impaired function. In such cases histological examinations show changes in the suprarenal cortex as well as in the suprarenal medulla. Taking this as a lead, the same changes have also been observed in feath-

Fur biting. Chinchilla with the typical "lion mane" as a result of fur biting.

er-biting birds. Since the function of the suprarenal is controlled by a gland at the base of the brain, the hypophysis, this was also examined and, indeed, in many cases it also displayed histological changes. Therefore fur biting is an impairment within the endocrine system and not a vice, as is often claimed. The results of the histological examination of actual cases studied were as follows:

— *hypophysis:* hyperplasia with distinct excess in eosinophyllic cells; knotted hyperplasia of the adenohypophysis;

— *suprarenal:* vacuolic, fatty degeneration of suprarenal cortex cells with dystrophic calcification; hyperplasia and degenerative fattiness of suprarenal structure; heart-shaped necrosis in suprarenal medulla.

Fur biting in chinchillas can also develop from one day to the next through stress situations when the animals are removed from their accustomed surroundings or when they are being disturbed. This is commonly seen following prolonged shipping, changes of enclosure or breeding room, and the

127

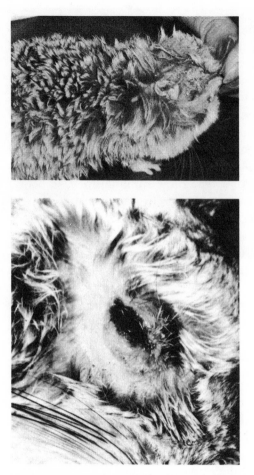

Severe fungus infections on a chinchilla head.

Skin and fur changes at the eye due to a fungus infection (*Trichophyton mentagrophytes*).

currently fashionable grooming of the pelt for shows. Breeders report that noise pollution, lack of ventilation, and damp breeding rooms can also trigger fur biting.

Treatment with ACTH or specific organ preparations is effective, but only for the duration of the therapy. Once this stops, fur biting resumes again. Other animals in the same enclosure or neighbors can actually learn fur biting!

## FUNGUS INFECTIONS

We are coming now to the last type of fur damage, which is of a totally different nature. It manifests itself in hair loss along the base of the tail or around the eyes in circular patterns. Sometimes this coincides with severe itching. The animal scratches and grooms itself continuously. Soon there is hair loss on the front paws and snout as well. If the animal is observed from one side (in profile) individual hairs appear shaved off. When these patches are then examined for fungus, one usually finds *Trichophyton mentagrophytes* or, much rarer, *Microsporum canis*. These are fungi that also occur on the skin of other mammals and on humans where they also cause hair loss in circular patches ("ring worm"). When and how the animals become infected is not known. There has to be a systemic susceptibility for these fungi and it is apparent that females seem to be more prone to it than males. Fungus attacks cannot be compared to regular infections since they are not necessarily passed on to other animals in the same enclosure. Basically these fungi cause a disease of the skin surface and associated hairs; therefore, medical treatment is indicated.

It is a fact that fungi are among those pathogens that are most strongly resistant to medication. Disinfectants usually fail completely; water and dampness actually encourage fungal growth. The normal ointments used on the skin are at best only temporary inhibitors to fungi. Concentrated alcohol is the most effective fungicide. Someone once had the bright idea of dipping chinchillas with fungus infections into 70% alcohol. We strongly believe that this is being cruel to animals! Should the animal survive, the fungi are most certainly dead, but there are many reports alleging that chinchillas have not survived this "treatment." In my experience in the field of fungus diseases in other mammals, it is completely adequate to rub or wash the affected areas with alcohol. A 1-2% salicylate alcohol has also proved to be quite effective in the treatment of skin fungus.

In addition, the pharmaceutical industry has produced a number of antimycotic drugs (fungus inhibitors) in the form of ointments, powders, and liquids, so that there is no lack of a specific therapy. Again, the fundamental preparation for successful treatment is shaving the affected hair areas.

The most modern antimycotic commercially available is Griseofulvin. The tablets are given orally and the chemical spreads in the bloodstream to the root of the hair as an inhibitor of fungal growth. Simultaneous external treatment of the affected areas with other medications will then kill off fungus on hairs. This method expedites healing and prevents pathogen transmission to other animals.

A word of warning: these substances must not be added aimlessly to the dust bath. Since chinchillas tend to feed on some of the dust they could also take in substantial amounts of these chemicals. It may be advisable to isolate the affected animals from the healthy ones. Moreover, animals with these skin diseases must not be treated simultaneously with antibiotics to treat some other disorder.

It has become an established practice among chinchilla breeders to treat fungus infestations with Ortozid mixed into the dust bath (1 teaspoon per bath for all animals in a breeding group). There are no reports published on this in veterinary medicine.

## SKIN PARASITES

Insects affecting chinchillas can be very effectively eradicated with insecticide impregnated plastic strips (pest strips,

Clothes moth (left), fur moth (center), and tapestry moth (right).

Fur moth larvae, lateral and dorsal views.

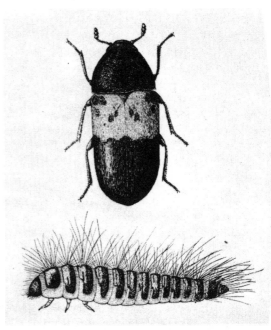

Dermestid beetle and larva.

Vapona) that are distributed around the breeding facility. These strips are suspended inside the breeding room in such a way that the animals cannot get into direct contact with them. A few hours later the room is insect-free. Pest strips cannot be used where there is no air circulation — follow label directions. The same principle is used for ectoparasites (lice and other hair-invading insects) in the fur of chinchillas, but here it is better to get as close as possible to the parasite. It has proved effective to place small pieces of pest strips to the cage in such a way that the animals cannot touch them. Within a few days the parasites will have disappeared. (To avoid possible toxic side effect, the pieces should be removed in three to five days.) This is an even better method than using a cat flea collar since the constant wearing tends to cause skin allergies. This method of parasite control has proved to be very effective in the husbandry of all sorts of mammals, and it is far superior than all other commercially available products, most notably those substances that must be washed or rubbed on, since they cannot be used on chinchillas.

# 9) Miscellaneous Topics

Euthanasia refers to the painless killing of a living being, with the emphasis on "painless." "Painless killing" is not related to the speed with which an animal dies. Instead, we have to know and understand the action of the killing agent on the body in order to be able to assess whether a rapid death is more painful than a slow, steady loss of consciousness followed by death or the reverse. There has been and still is much discussion about effective, painless euthanasia methods, and many methods are praised as being the most effective and most humane.

One possible method (when executed correctly) is cervical dislocation (neck fracture) as practiced in mink breeding. But not everybody can bring himself to do that. The human spirit of invention has produced killing devices of all sorts and formats and the means employed are equally diverse. We must retain sight of the fact that euthanasia of chinchillas is being done by laymen and therefore it must be simple and totally effective. It is impossible to go to a veterinarian with each individual animal for a lethal injection. Not all euthanasia methods available can be discussed here in detail, but those that are acceptable in terms of animal welfare aspects and from the point of view of a veterinarian must be mentioned here.

Basically, suitable gases or liquids that anesthetize and kill in their gaseous form, such as carbon dioxide and chloroform, can be good euthanasia agents. Most of these are anesthetics that become lethal only when given as an overdose. When such agents are used it is important to make sure that the container is completely air-tight — escaping gas could endanger man and animal (nearly all of these substances are highly flammable), and even a small amount of fresh air entering the container can simulate apparent death (suspended animation) from which the animal recovers.

Agents that cause suffocation, such as hydrocyanic acid, natural gas, or other poisons, are to be categorically rejected since their use would indeed constitute cruelty. Electrocution must also be rejected for similar reasons.

From a veterinary point of view all those euthanasia methods that utilize overdoses of anesthetics are acceptable in terms of animal welfare considerations. These injections can, for instance, consist of 20% chloral hydrate solution given into the abdominal cavity or suitable narcotics. In other cases chinchillas are injected intramuscular with a sedative and after this has taken effect a euthanasia agent such as T 61 is injected into the heart.

When using carbon dioxide as a euthanizing agent, the animal will become immediately unconscious and dies painlessly while in this state. It must be pointed out here that carbon dioxide is odorless and must be handled cautiously. If there is a leakage, anyone handling the gas may be at risk while breathing this gas.

## DISINFECTION

Disinfection is the most important means of preventing the spread of diseases. Although this has already been emphasized earlier, some additional, more explicit comments appear relevant.

Disinfectants must never be used under conditions and in situations where they can harm man or animal. All disinfectants have some corrosive properties and can cause serious damage to skin and mucous membranes. There is substantial evidence that disinfectants are not always used properly. The most important prerequisite for an effective disinfection is thorough cleaning of cage, enclosures, and equipment. It is totally wrong to use disinfectants on dirty objects. Instead, everything should be washed in hot water and detergent first, followed by disinfection with a recognized product. Caustic soda, Lysol, quaternary ammonium bases, and many others have been tried out.

Disinfectants must be given ample time to work, after which they are washed off with *lots of water;* there must not be any residual chemicals left on equipment or cages. In the event of heavily infected stocks it is advisable to repeat this procedure at short intervals. If afterward the enclosures and cages can be left empty for some time (one to four weeks), this aids the disinfection process by withholding nutrients from infectious pathogens.

If really strong disinfection is needed — to combat virus infections, for instance — cages and equipment should be steam-cleaned or burned off with a blowtorch. All items to be disinfected must first be properly washed. The most modern method is spraying disinfectants, which has proved to be quite effective. The tiny droplets penetrate all openings (cracks, crevices, holes), which is more thorough than merely scrubbing with a brush. It can be said that with disinfection, as with other things in life, it is thoroughness that brings success.

## IMPORTANT DATA

– *Body temperature* (taken with a standard rectal thermometer for three minutes): in male chinchillas, 35.8°C (96.4°F); in females, on the average, 35.4°C (97.5°F), varying from 36° to 38°C (96.8°-100°F).

– *Heat or estrus* in females: normally from the age of three or four months, every 28 to 30 days. Externally visible by means of an open vagina, which stays open for three to four days.

– *Gestation period:* in *Chinchilla lanigera*, 111 days; in *C. brevicaudata*, 128 days. Variations of five days can occur. Usually one to five embryos are carried to full term.

– *Blood data (hematology):* About 10 million red blood cells (9-12 million); white blood cells about 10,000/cmm. Hemoglobin: 75 to 101 H.U. or 12-16.2 g%. Differentiation, on the average, 1.5% eosinophilic and 30 to 40% neutrophilic granulocytes, 53% lymphycytes, and 1.5% monocytes; on the average, 2% are early (immature) stages. Therefore chinchillas have a lymphocytic blood picture.

134

– *Anesthesia: Thiogenal* appears to be the most *effective anesthetizing agent.* Healthy animals are given 80 mg/kg body weight (5% solution) intraperitoneally; other authors recommend only 50 mg/kg. *Ether anesthetic* has been used with success ·by various veterinarians. Ketanest, Vetalar: short-acting (about 30 minutes) anesthetic that can be used without risks. 20 mg/kg body weight intramuscular (concentration levels must be complied with!); supplement injections possible.

– *X-ray values* for a complete exposure: 50 mA: 55 kV:0.1 sec; with film without grid.

# Medications

This is only a partial listing of those medications that, mainly in my own experience, have proved to be effective in chinchillas. It needs to be further expanded and completed as new data and test results become available. Many of these drug names are used internationally, but others are European and will have to be researched by your veterinarian to find the local equivalent or generic drug.

*Acranil:* Used against single-celled organisms; 25 mg/day/animal, given over food, for three to five days.

*ACTH:* Hypophysis hormone; 1.6 I.U., injected intramuscularly.

*Antibiotics:* Available in all forms, injectable as aqueous or oil-based solutions, as capsules and tablets, in powder form, and as syrups; also for local application as powders and suspensions. Manufactured by a great number of pharmaceutical companies. Penicillin and streptomycin are the oldest antibiotics, but are currently no longer used in chinchillas. Acromycin, Aureomycin, Hostacycline, and Terramycin (the broad-spectrum antibiotics) are all tetracycline derivatives. They are used predominantly as capsules given orally, but they are also available as tablets, syrup, and injectable solutions. Chinchillas should *not* be given more than 25 mg/day per animal. Possibly supplement with sulfonamide. Monitor for disorder of intestinal flora!

A reminder: a prolonged oral administration of tetracycline

must be supplemented with vitamin B or yeast.

Chloramphenicol is the most effective antibiotic for chinchillas. Trade names for it include Chloromycetin and Paraxin. Only to be given as suspension or orally (never as an injected solution). Colistin is particularly effective against gastrointestinal diseases.

Antimycotics (fungus inhibiting agents): Multifungin, Chlorisept, Herpetren, Likuden M, Fulcin S, Griseofulvin. These substances are available in liquid and powdered forms and as ointments and tablets.

*AT 10:* Hydrated tachysterin; corresponds to the effect of the parathyroid hormone. As drops, in capsules, and in oily solution usable for injections. Once, 0.2 to 0.5 ml, intramuscular or as drops.

*Calcium:* Most effective as injections; for chinchillas use only calcium preparations that can be injected under the skin. Calcium-Sandoz 10%, Calphon, and others; 0.5 ml under the skin, repeat as needed after one to two days.

*Carnigen:* Medication to act on circulatory system; as drops or twice daily ¼ to ½ tablet. Easily compatible and very effective.

*Chinchilla Immunization,* quintuplicate: 0.5 ml subcutaneously — two vaccinations in intervals of two to three weeks for animals older than 12 weeks; one booster vaccination annually.

*Chin-Vac:* Mixed vaccine against the most common infections in chinchillas. Juveniles under 30 days, 0.1 ml intramuscularly; two to four months of age, 0.2 ml intramuscularly; from four months onward, 0.2-.25 ml intramuscularly. Three injections at intervals of about ten days (consult manufacturer's instructions).

*Chinosol (Quinosol):* Oral prophylactic, primarily to inhibit or limit oral infections. Yellow tablets to be dissolved as per manufacturer's instructions.

*Chlorethyl Spray:* Used for localized freezing anesthesia in minor surgery.

*Chloral Hydrate:* White crystals; in 20% solution to euthanize chinchillas, injected into abdominal cavity.

*Chloramphenicol (Chloromycetin, Leucomycin,* or *Praxin:* Antibiotics.

136

*Coecolysin:* Used against cholic-type disorders; 0.5 ml under the skin. Can be repeated after a few hours.

*Colistin:* Up to 50,000 units per animal per day intramuscularly or orally.

*Coli Mixed Vaccine:* Vaccine to immunize chinchillas via the drinking water.

*Crescovit:* Protective liver therapy. Similar action from Aminotylon, Methionin, and others. 0.5 ml injected under the skin every other day.

*Disinfection:* Only a few substances are mentioned here; others may be used if tested by experts. Caustic soda, sagrotan, lyson, lysolin, quaternary ammonium bases.

*Erythromycin (Erycinum, Ilotycin):* Broad-spectrum antibiotic. Should only be used after pathogen (resistance) testing.

*Glucocorticoids (Cortison, Scheroson, Prednison, Prednisolon):* The same effects as adrenocortical hormone (ACTH). Various forms of injectable preparations, also as ointments, eye drops, and tablets. Application must be strictly monitored.

*Hypophysin:* Very effective ecbolic; 0.8 to 1 unit under the skin, can be repeated after one to two hours.

*Insecticides (Contact):* To eradicate ectoparasites (fleas, lice, mites, etc.). Neguvon, Jakutin, or other hexachlorcyclohexanes. Supplied as liquid, powder, or emulsion. *CAUTION:* Animals must not be permitted to lick themselves after application, since the active ingredients can cause gastrointestinal inflammation and liver damage. Large amounts taken internally can be fatal!

*Isocaine 2%, Xylocaine:* For use as local anesthetics. As needed, injected or sprayed on.

*Ketanest:* Effective sedative. 20 to 80 mg active ingredient/kg body weight intramuscularly. Concentrations must be closely controlled! Injections can be repeated.

*Milk of Bismuth:* Suspension of bismuth hydroxide and bismuth subcarbonate; to neutralize digestive juices of the stomach; antidiarrheal. As required, one pinch (tip of knife blade) daily into food or in liquid via pipette. *Bismuth subnitrate* is a very effective antidiarrheal drug but not an antacid.

*Miragest:* Mineral mixture administered via food.

*Nasal Drops:* Catarrh of the upper respiratory tract. Same medications as used in pediatrics. One drop every second day into the nose.

*Novalgin:* Relieves cramps (spasms); in tablet form or as injection. 0.1 to 0.2 ml intramuscularly; must NOT be given subcutaneously!

*Ointments and Pastes:* For treatment of minor, non-infected wounds or for eczema, use cod liver oil ointment and similar products. If wounds are infected or dirty, use antibiotic or sulfonamide ointments or combinations. The following have proven to be particularly effective: Supronal Emulsion and Supracillin Suspension; the latter has strong granulating properties.

*Oralpaedon:* Dissolved in water and as liquid; electrolyte replacement.

*Oxytocin (ORASTIN):* Ecbolic (increase contractions during delivery and to aid passage of afterbirth).

*Paraffin Oil (Kerosene):* For the treatment of constipation; orally via pipette (0.5 to 1 ml), as well as enema.

*Perlacar:* As injection for skin diseases (about twice weekly) to support localized treatment.

*Powders:* For wound treatment; all non-differentiated, non-perfumed body and wound powders.

*Sulfonamide (Sulfamethazine):* Given either as injections, tablets, or in drinking water. Injections should be of low concentrations (7.5%), intramuscularly.

*Sympatol:* For cardiac and circulatory weakness (one to two drops).

*Tetracycline:* Antibiotic; tends to disturb the intestinal flora within a short period of time, therefore should only be given for three days. Related preparations are Achromycin, chlortetracycline, Aureomycin, oxytetracycline, Terramycin.

*T 61:* Euthanizing agent: must only be used after anesthesia has been induced!

*Thibenzole:* Antiparasitic effective against a number of endoparasites (worms, single-celled organisms). Each animal receives about 6-8 gr of active ingredient. WARNING: the concentration of some commercial products is 50%!

*Veriazole:* Circulatory medication with good compatibility; as drops or under the skin, 0.1 to 0.2 ml.

*Vitamins:*

*A:* For skin and mucous membrane disorders, given locally

as drops, orally, or intramuscularly.

*B-Complex:* General systemic support, for nerve damage, and to re-establish intestinal flora. 100 mg intramuscularly or 1-2 tablets Betabion Forte daily.

*C:* Has proved to be particularly effective as support therapy for respiratory diseases. 100 mg intramuscularly.

*D:* General systemic support. 10,000 units intramuscularly, tablets and drops. Vigantol is very popular, given either orally or as injection, and D-Mulsion orally. Prolonged administration only in conjunction with calcium.

*E:* To improve fertility and to strengthen the heart muscle. Evio, E-Mulsin, and others. Daily drops or injected intramuscularly.

*K:* Important factor for blood coagulation; to be used accordingly.

*T:* Not a vitamin; out-dated term.

*Vitamin Dosages:*
A-Mulsin: 1 drop every 2nd day, orally.
B (Betabion, Betaxin): 100 mg/animal/day, orally or i.m.
Cebion: 100 mg/animal/day, i.m.
D-Mulsin: 1 drop every 2nd day, orally.
E-Mulsin: 1 drop every 2nd day, orally.
Multi-Mulsin: 1 drop every 2nd day, orally.

# Index

Chinchillas are relatively easy to maintain as healthy, contented animals, provided their owners really appreciate them and give them the care they deserve.